CONTAINER GARDENING
The Permaculture Way

Sustainably Grow
VEGETABLES & MORE
in Your Small Space

VALÉRY TSIMBA
Translated by LUCINDA KARTER

THE EXPERIMENT

NEW YORK

Container Gardening—The Permaculture Way: *Sustainably Grow Vegetables and More in Your Small Space*

Text and photographs copyright © 2021 by Les Éditions Eugen Ulmer, Paris, France
Photographs on pages iv, 2, 4, 24–25, 41, 42, 51, 65, 77, 103, 142–43, and 147 (top and bottom) copyright © 2021 by Evaine Merle
Photograph on page 26, and author photograph, copyright © 2021 by Paul Cheam
Translation copyright © 2024 by The Experiment, LLC

Originally published in France as *Mon balcon nourricier en permaculture* by Éditions Ulmer in 2021. First published in North America in English by The Experiment, LLC, in 2024.

The Experiment, LLC
220 East 23rd Street, Suite 600
New York, NY 10010-4658
theexperimentpublishing.com

THE EXPERIMENT and its colophon are registered trademarks of The Experiment, LLC. Many of the designations used by manufacturers and sellers to distinguish their products are claimed as trademarks. Where those designations appear in this book and The Experiment was aware of a trademark claim, the designations have been capitalized.

The Experiment's books are available at special discounts when purchased in bulk for premiums and sales promotions as well as for fundraising or educational use. For details, contact us at info@theexperimentpublishing.com.

Library of Congress Cataloging-in-Publication Data available upon request

ISBN 978-1-891011-38-2
Ebook ISBN 978-1-891011-39-9

Cover design by Beth Bugler
Text design by Jack Dunnington
Translation by Lucinda Karter

Manufactured in China

First printing April 2024
10 9 8 7 6 5 4 3 2 1

CONTENTS

INTRODUCTION

My name is Valéry, and I'm the happy owner of a balcony vegetable garden and two window boxes in Paris, France's most densely populated metropolitan area. Seeds are my passion and I take great pleasure in planting and watching them grow in an edible garden that nourishes my body and soul.

I've been passionate about plants ever since the age of 10, when I spent time at a summer camp in the Alps. We took part in nature activities every day, and it was during one of our many forest hikes that I fell in love with plants. Little did I know then that a different kind of seed had been planted in me, although it would lay dormant for many years. It was only once I had settled into my first apartment that it took hold and began to grow. I started gardening in window boxes, growing traditional geraniums and a few herbs, until I finally owned my own apartment with a balcony twelve years later in 2005.

In the meantime, visits to friends who had vegetable gardens in the countryside helped to maintain and nourish my passion. I began borrowing gardening books from the library and watching videos on YouTube. With their help, I was able to quench my thirst for gardening knowledge.

In 2013, I gained access to a small plot in a community garden—my first time planting in the ground. As the years went by, both my enthusiasm and experience grew. I discovered permaculture, and my ardent desire to (re)connect with what I ate inspired me to start a balcony garden, where I cultivate dozens of plants that constitute part of my diet all year long. My balcony is small and narrow—about 2 feet by 22 feet (0.6 m x 6 m)—and I naturally gravitated toward permaculture and corresponding techniques that allowed me to foster abundance in a small space. The size of my balcony could easily have been an obstacle, but it turned out to be a stroke of luck because it forced me to be creative. Gardening is all at once a game, a pleasure, and a rich apprenticeship.

In March 2020, during the COVID-19 lockdown, it was my little balcony garden that gave me some autonomy when my food co-op shut down. My balcony garden allowed me to harvest lettuce, arugula, mizuna, kale, Swiss chard, sorrel, and endive that was fresh, full of flavor, and rich in nutrients. This balcony, already a source of fresh air in the city—literally and figuratively—took on far greater importance.

Growing a container vegetable garden is simple to do and is accessible to anyone with a bit of outdoor space, whether you have a balcony like I do, a window box, a patio, or a strip of driveway. All it takes is a little patience, careful observation, and motivation. I truly hope that my experience will give you the desire, curiosity, and enthusiasm to start your own container garden, no matter the size.

You'll see—everything you grow will have extraordinary flavor.

WHAT IS PERMACULTURE?

Permaculture, a contraction of "permanent agriculture," is at once a philosophy and a way of life that aims to build durable and resilient human structures by taking cues from natural ecosystems. This philosophy can be applied to different aspects of life, such as health and well-being, finance, education, culture, habitat, tools, technology, and more. Permaculture is less a gardening technique than a toolbox for approaching the design and cultivation of a garden that is productive, healthy, resilient, and self-regulated.

Permaculture philosophy was developed in the 1970s in Australia by Bill Mollison and David Holmgren, and it rests on three fundamental ethics, or more practically speaking, reasons why someone might want to use permaculture in their garden design.

1. **To care for the earth**
2. **To care for humankind**
3. **To limit one's consumption and create and share abundance**

You don't need a lot of space to create abundance. While you may not be able to produce enough food to fulfill all the nutritional needs for one person, let alone a family, you'll get to enjoy the flavor and satisfaction of eating homegrown produce. By creating abundance, you are also providing a home for aphids, ladybugs, hoverflies, butterflies, and bees, and establishing a green oasis for birds. The magic of permaculture is that we can care for ourselves and our nutritional needs by growing edible plants while at the same time caring for the local fauna, no matter where you live.

PERMACULTURE IN CONTAINERS?

Using the word "permaculture" in relation to container gardening might, in the strictest sense, feel like a stretch. After all, the "perma" part of the word derives from "permanent." Growing plants in containers or small raised beds, often in rented accommodation, is usually less permanent than more traditional permaculture models of building a food forest in the ground.

But stripped back to its barest elements, permaculture is a design toolbox and worldview that can be applied to any space—even a window box! In-ground gardening, on a large or even small scale, is simply not possible for millions of people, whether because of where they live, the amount of time and money they have, disability, or many other factors.

The permaculture-inspired principles in this book focus not on treating nature as disposable but on participating in the relationships that plants and other living beings like birds, insects, and fungi have with each other. A few strawberries and herbs growing in your window box might feel completely disconnected from the wider ecosystem, but you will be surprised to learn that there are creative ways to integrate your container garden, in any shape and form, and the way you tend it, into the ecosystem around you. You can use the movement of water, air, heat, and nutrients through your neighborhood to grow food in less wasteful ways that nurture the health of the wider world and the creatures who share it with you.

Most gardeners, even those who also undertake in-ground gardening (including myself!) use containers in their gardens in some way. I think many would like to think more holistically and ecologically about the way they garden in containers but may not know where to start, since most eco-friendly horticultural resources are directed at in-ground gardening. My hope is to invite readers to have rewarding, caring relationships with the natural world through container gardening, no matter where you may be gardening or how long you may be able to do so in that one place.

Bee flying toward a sunflower

PERMACULTURE AS A SOURCE OF INSPIRATION

When Bill Mollison, David Holmgren, and their colleagues started articulating permaculture as a system in the 1970s, they weren't creating something from scratch. They were deeply informed by the patterns of living with and from the land, practiced by Aboriginal Australians for millennia.

The Twelve Core Principles of Permaculture that Mollison and Holmgren laid out decades ago are to this day just as relevant to a container garden as a multi-acre enterprise. Here are examples of all twelve principles as I have adapted them for my own container garden.

Observe and Interact

I observe my vegetable garden daily so I don't miss the slightest change in any of the plants, and therefore I notice when a plant may be happier in one location than another. Before starting my vegetable garden, I went through an observation phase, noting the space, size, and layout of my balcony; its sun exposure and wind conditions; and the types of insects and birds that visit it, so I could get the most out of its resources.

Obtain a Yield

This principle of permaculture is an essential one that gives me a sense of purpose and has motivated me to grow a more productive vegetable garden over the years, regardless of the fact that I have only a small amount of space.

Collect and Store Energy

By gardening on my balcony, I use the sun's energy (see page 21 for more about how sunlight affects plants). The sun is a key player in photosynthesis, a process that enables plants to build organic matter by absorbing carbon dioxide and emitting oxygen. I plant densely so that the thick foliage can take advantage of all the sunlight that falls on my balcony and conserve the water around their roots. I also set up containers in key places to capture rainwater for later use.

Use Renewable Resources and Energy

This principle encourages me to use what I have at hand. Rather than buying mulch, I use my plant's byproducts to mulch my containers, where earthworms break down the mulch into fertilizer over time. In fact, many of my containers were someone else's trash that I rescued and repurposed.

Let Nothing Go to Waste

All the "waste" I produce in my vegetable garden stays there. What's left over from pruning or other growing waste becomes mulch or compost (more on this on page 72). Sometimes I add my kitchen scraps directly to the top of my containers when my composter is full or if there is no option to drop waste off at my community garden or in collection bins around my neighborhood, as was the case during the early days of the COVID-19 pandemic.

Self-Regulate and Accept Feedback

I let my vegetable garden self-regulate. Following a massive invasion of aphids in the spring of 2020, rather than use insecticides or pesticides—even natural ones—I let the ladybugs and their larvae do the job. It's true that it may take time for aphids' predators to arrive on the scene, but I always depend on nature's self-regulation. I summon my patience and wait.

Start with Big Patterns; Work Down to Small Details

The idea behind this principle is to be mindful that a garden, even one planted in multiple separate containers, is a connected system. Look at what works for the whole rather than the separate parts. How do sun and wind and water move throughout the whole space? Based on this, I take my inspiration from forest ecosystems and arrange my plants by size, starting with the largest ones, planting the medium-sized ones around them, and finishing with small plants like lettuce for ground cover, so every plant has access to sunlight. Thoughtful arrangement can also create beneficial "microclimates." For example, a tall tomato plant can create a shady microclimate for basil planted nearby.

Every Part of the System Must Serve More Than One Purpose

The addition of flowers to a vegetable garden has several functions. Flowers are pleasant to look at and they add a pleasing aesthetic. Some of them, like marigolds, keep predatory insects at bay. Others feed pollinators thanks to their pollen and/or nectar. Finally, some produce seeds that birds find delectable.

Integrate Rather Than Segregate

As long as plants aren't going to crowd each other out, there's no reason you can't mix different kinds of herbs, flowers, and vegetables all in the same container, a technique often known as polyculture. In fact, plants usually benefit from this! I practice the technique of companion planting, finding homes for plants according to the mutual support they offer each other. For example, I plant carrots next to members of the allium family, such as garlic, leeks, or onions, as they fend off carrot flies. Carrots, in turn, repulse leek moths. (These particular pests are more of a problem in Europe than America, but many companion plantings can help with plant issues local to you. You can read more about polyculture and companion planting on page 68.)

Use and Value Diversity

This principle, which echoes the one before, is an invitation to diversify your crops—and therefore the creatures that you welcome into your garden space—in order to confront, among other things, diseases specific to certain plants.

I usually grow several aromatic plants, whose strong odors confuse pests, next to the plants that attract those pests. I also grow flowers that repel or trap pests. For example, fava beans are susceptible to black bean aphids, so in spring, I sow nasturtium seeds between the bean plants, and the nasturtiums attract the aphids away from the beans.

Start Small and Go Slow

Just because you're working in a small space doesn't mean you have to fill the whole thing with plants in a single season. In fact, trying to do so may overwhelm you and leave you with nothing instead of a modest start that teaches and inspires you.

Growing a small balcony vegetable garden is a simple way to supplement my diet and to connect to the rhythm of nature throughout the seasons. In the hustle and bustle of urban life, growing a vegetable garden is a great way to slow down, to marvel at the beauty and magic of life, and to develop patience and access calm.

Value the Marginal

In nature, the meeting of two ecosystems gives rise to greater biodiversity and increased productivity. Where two ecosystems like a forest and a meadow overlap, we find plants and animals that are adapted to each as well as those that are adapted to the space in between.

In cities, marginal areas like roads, urban fringes, parks, balconies, and even windowsills act as boundaries between different environments, and in some cases, as microecosystems of their own. Growing a vegetable garden on my balcony, the marginal space between my apartment and the outside, enables me to create a biodiverse zone that provides me with food and helps bring nature back to the city.

And One Bonus Principle: The Only Limit Is Your Imagination

This principle comes from a quote by Bill Mollinson. I like to think of gardening as a creative act. It helps to liberate my imagination from normative ideas and inspires me to reach toward other horizons and to think outside the box.

Borage flowers produce nectar for pollinators.

SOME TOOLS FROM THE PERMACULTURE TOOLBOX

Zones

Not to be confused with USDA Hardiness Zones, permaculture uses the word "zones" to describe how different areas of land are utilized. The traditional permaculture zones are as follows.

- **Zone 0:** House, dwelling, or other buildings

- **Zone 1:** Areas that you continually observe and/or pass through

- **Zone 2:** Less intensively cultivated or managed areas

- **Zone 3:** Occasionally visited areas that are nevertheless part of the permaculture system

- **Zone 4:** Wild areas for foraging food, fuel, or other materials

- **Zone 5:** Natural unmanaged areas (forest, fields, etc.)

In your container garden, you'll need to shrink your perspective, but you can still find many if not all of these zones! Some examples from my own balcony garden include the following.

- **Zones 0 and 1:** These often merge at different times of day or year when space is tight. I might use my kitchen surfaces for cooking meals but also for sorting seeds and growing sprouts.

- **Zone 1:** This includes the trays of seedlings on my windowsill that I check on every morning and evening, or particularly tender plants in my container garden that need daily attention.

- **Zone 2:** In my garden, this zone is made up of the established mature plants that I water several times a week, but that I might not look at closely every single day.

- **Zones 3 and 4:** My community compost heap and the places down the block where I collect fallen leaves are integral parts of my system, even though they are spatially separated from my balcony.

- **Zone 5:** While I don't personally cultivate the flowers and trees in my neighbors' gardens—and even though these aren't wild, unmanaged spaces—their natural seasonal signals are integral to my gardening patterns. Just as important, these natural areas sustain living beings—insects, birds, fungi, bacteria, and more—that also visit and benefit my garden.

Zone 00

Landscapes and climates are diverse, and so are gardeners. In recent years, some permaculture thinkers have used the idea of Zone 00 to think about the internal or embodied realities of gardeners themselves. Other practitioners think of the gardener more as a "sector," or force that moves across zones. Paying attention to your role in your garden ecosystem can mean cultivating a personal ethic of care or educating yourself more about interconnectedness. But it can also mean thinking holistically about your own health or disability, financial position, or workload.

Container gardening can be accessible to people for whom traditional in-ground gardening might be difficult or impossible. If we understand that humans are not separate from nature, it makes sense that limited physical mobility, lack of funds to buy land, or shortage of time due to caring for a family member are all as relevant to a garden system as sun exposure or days of winter frost.

For example, housing insecurity might mean you need to plant in several smaller containers rather than one or two large ones (see "Containers" on page 28). You'll need to water your plants more frequently and there may be a few varieties you can't grow, but you'll also be able to take them with you if you suddenly need to move mid-season. Gardening this way goes against most advice you'll read about how to choose containers, but it's very much in keeping with the permaculture principle to start with big patterns and work down to small details.

We can also understand that the help of other people who are not the "primary gardener" can be as necessary to a flourishing garden as insects or seasonal rains. One gardener living with ME/CFS (myalgic encephalomyelitis/chronic fatigue syndrome) described how, when she is on bedrest, family members carry a few potted plants to her bedroom windowsill so she can still care for them even when she can't go outside. Another disabled gardener revealed how she encourages people to think about the ways that different weather and climates can affect their ability to work in the garden. Heat intolerance or chronic pain triggered by sudden changes in weather may mean that your garden is flourishing while you are suffering. If you know what weather can be triggering for you, you can talk to friends or neighbors about possible help with plant care as you plan your garden.

It's less important whether you call human life factors zones or sectors (or neither) than it is to think about them while planning your garden and to be as open to the seasons of your life and body as you are to nature's.

Sectors

In permaculture, the term "sectors" is used to describe natural or uncontrolled influences, forces, or energies that move through your growing space. These can include sunlight, wind, weather, pollution, noise, and many more. While you can't control these forces directly, by observing and analyzing your growing space, you can understand them and respond to them appropriately. Depending on the sector, you might take steps to divert or reduce its effects or even channel and make use of them.

Here are some examples of sectors in a theoretical uncovered, southwest-facing patio garden in a condominium complex, along with examples of how a gardener could creatively use, divert, or reduce the forces.

- Bright glare on summer mornings when the sunrise reflects off the glass-paneled building across the street—a tub of tomato plants, thickly leafed out by midsummer, will appreciate the heat and light and will shade more delicate plants

- Dappled shade from a sidewalk tree in July—beneficial for tender leafy greens that would survive longer into the first summer heat wave than they would on a patio that doesn't get any shade

- Hot, dry air from the neighbor's air conditioner exhaust vent—during the hottest part of summer, a tub of tough prairie plants that pollinators love like grasses and succulents can handle this corner, provided they're given extra water to help them cope. The tall grasses shield other plants from the full force of the blast.

- The toddler next door loves to chuck toys over your railing . . . again and again and again—a friendly conversation with the toddler's family lets them know why you're putting up a mesh screen at this end of the patio to protect your plants!

- Heavy rains—set out extra tubs and buckets to collect this valuable resource for drier times

- Curious squirrels living in nearby trees like to dig in pots—planting onions around the outside edge makes digging less tempting to squirrels, but a bit of chicken wire and focused application of cayenne pepper after rain can help when plants are young and delicate

- Asphalt floor gets extremely hot when exposed to full sun—covering the surface with as much planting as possible shields the asphalt and protects roots. Some natural matting can also help temper the asphalt's ability to absorb heat

- Slow release of afternoon warmth on winter and spring days from the brick wall at the back of the patio—a potted perennial shrub moves against the brick all winter to keep its roots from freezing, and the corner gives seedlings a gentle start every spring

Get in the Zone

Whatever the extremes of your climate, keep in mind that containers exaggerate those extremes by raising plants away from the ground. Roots lifted above the soil line (as they are in containers) freeze and overheat more easily than roots in surrounding soil. Soil raised above ground level will also dry out before the ground beneath it does. Plant roots "imprisoned" by the walls of a pot won't be able to travel in search of water and nutrients the way they would in open ground. Rest assured, none of this makes a container garden impossible, or even more work, than an in-ground garden. It's just a matter of getting to know your micro-environment, and learning to think like plants do.

The USDA Plant Hardiness Zones map and the associated first and last average frost dates by zone are useful starting places to learn about your local environment, and any quality seeds you buy in North America will come with instructions about the best time to sow them in relation to your average frost dates.

In addition to average frost dates or rainfall, it can be illuminating to look back through actual local data from recent years by checking your ZIP Code (freely available on climate.gov). You'll probably be surprised by how much the weather can vary from year to year! Knowing how much variation is possible can prime you to be an observant, curious gardener who doesn't take temperature or rainfall for granted. In the US, the Cooperative Extension System is also an incredible resource providing free, hyperlocal growing and climate information. A quick Google search of your state and the words "cooperative extension service" will help locate extension services closest to you.

Keep in mind that the acceleration of climate change means that many average frost dates and low temperatures reflected by the USDA Plant Hardiness Zone map are changing faster than new guidance can be issued. The map is still a good place to start, but vigilance with monitoring weather forecasts and connecting with other gardeners in your neighborhood to compare observations and experiences is more important than ever before.

USDA Agricultural Research Service
U.S. DEPARTMENT OF AGRICULTURE

Seattle
OLYMPIA
Spokane
Portland
SALEM
Columbia
Medford
HELENA
Billings
BOISE
Pocatello
Elko
CARSON CITY
SACRAMENTO
San Francisco
Fresno
Las Vegas
Saint George
Los Angeles
San Diego
PHOENIX
Flagstaff
Tucson
Missouri
Minot
BISMARCK
PIERRE
Rapid City
Casper
CHEYENNE
Kearney
DENVER
Grand Junction
Colorado
SANTA FE
Albuquerque
Amarillo
Midland
El Paso
Rio Grande
San Antonio
AUS
Siou

Hawaii
HONOLULU

0 25 50 100
Miles
Kilometers
0 38 75 150

Alaska
Fairbanks
Anchorage
JUNEAU

0 70 140 280
Miles
Kilometers
0 105 210 420

0 75 150
0 100 200

USDA Plant Hardiness Zones

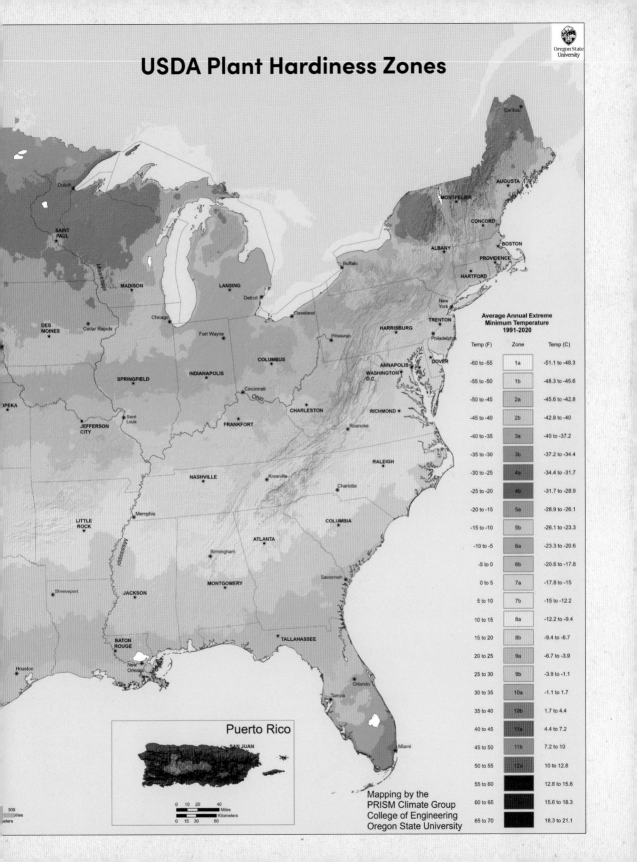

Oregon State University

Average Annual Extreme Minimum Temperature 1991-2020

Temp (F)	Zone	Temp (C)
-60 to -55	1a	-51.1 to -48.3
-55 to -50	1b	-48.3 to -45.6
-50 to -45	2a	-45.6 to -42.8
-45 to -40	2b	-42.8 to -40
-40 to -35	3a	-40 to -37.2
-35 to -30	3b	-37.2 to -34.4
-30 to -25	4a	-34.4 to -31.7
-25 to -20	4b	-31.7 to -28.9
-20 to -15	5a	-28.9 to -26.1
-15 to -10	5b	-26.1 to -23.3
-10 to -5	6a	-23.3 to -20.6
-5 to 0	6b	-20.6 to -17.8
0 to 5	7a	-17.8 to -15
5 to 10	7b	-15 to -12.2
10 to 15	8a	-12.2 to -9.4
15 to 20	8b	-9.4 to -6.7
20 to 25	9a	-6.7 to -3.9
25 to 30	9b	-3.9 to -1.1
30 to 35	10a	-1.1 to 1.7
35 to 40	10b	1.7 to 4.4
40 to 45	11a	4.4 to 7.2
45 to 50	11b	7.2 to 10
50 to 55	12a	10 to 12.8
55 to 60	12b	12.8 to 15.6
60 to 65	13a	15.6 to 18.3
65 to 70	13b	18.3 to 21.1

Puerto Rico

SAN JUAN

0 10 20 40 Miles
0 15 30 60 Kilometers

Mapping by the
PRISM Climate Group
College of Engineering
Oregon State University

Heat and Cold

While tall buildings and tightly packed apartment dwellings pose a challenge when it comes to allowing residents enough space to build a garden, an urban environment can also help moderate cold winter temperatures. Stone, brick, and tall walls accumulate heat during the day and release it back into the environment overnight, meaning that if you live in downtown Minneapolis or Montreal (USDA Zones 4 and 5, respectively), your overnight winter temperatures might be milder than someone who lives 20 miles outside the city limits, though technically still in the same Hardiness Zone.

However, if residing in a Hardiness Zone lower than 6 or 7, you might be hard-pressed to find plants that can survive your winters unsheltered in containers. Having a well-sealed garage, shed, or cool basement to house potted plants during cold months can go a long way in keeping them alive. Keep in mind that most temperate perennials (like a dwarf apple tree, for instance) need their season of winter dormancy, so bringing them into your heated apartment during the winter months won't be viable. One workaround for this can be to grow tender perennials, like citrus trees, lavender, or rosemary, that are used to not going fully dormant and can therefore tolerate a winter vacation in a heated house, assuming you have a cool window to keep them by that provides enough light and moisture levels in the air.

Urban environments' abilities to hold heat—which can be so helpful in the winter—can put plants under more stress in summer. You might have to do more in summer to help your plants withstand the heat than would another container gardener just 50 miles (80 km) away in a less densely populated and paved environment. Growing larger plants that cast shade, using shade cloths, and even moving containers inside on especially hot days can all help with heat stress.

No matter your overall zone, the more hot days without rain you have in a given summer, the more water-challenged your plants' roots will be. In some cases, even with sufficient water, roots can overheat if the pots they're growing in receive direct sunlight, and in extreme conditions, for multiple hours a day.

By finding the biggest growing container you can, mulching heavily, and grouping containers together, you'll be able to create better insulation for root systems, which will keep plants happier in both hot *and* cold conditions.

You may also choose to grow specific heat-resistant or cold-hardy vegetables as appropriate. Some heat-resistant vegetables include okra, sweet and hot peppers, eggplant, tomatillo, Cape gooseberry, tomato, cucumber, onion, leek, summer squash, pumpkin ('Jack Be Little' works well in small spaces), carrot, beet, beans, sweet potato, potato, Swiss chard, kale, collards, and amaranth. Some cold-hardy vegetables include brussels sprouts, cabbage, kale, cauliflower, collards, leek, rutabaga, carrot, parsnip, sorrel, mâché, Swiss chard, and spinach.

SUN EXPOSURE

Before you decide what you're going to grow in your container garden, you need to figure out what primary direction your space faces, or its exposure. This is fundamental because the strength of sunlight differs between north, south, east, and west, and different plants need different amounts of light to reach their full potential, grow harmoniously, and be productive.

North

In the northern hemisphere, a northern exposure receives the least number of hours of direct sunlight. Shadows cast by walls and buildings can further reduce the hours of direct sunlight available in an urban garden or even in a large backyard. However, as long as you get at least 4 hours of direct sunlight a day, you have some options.

For a north-facing garden with at least 4 hours of sunlight, choose leafy vegetables like lettuce, spinach, arugula, or Asian greens such as bok choy, Napa cabbage, mizuna, mibuna, and komatsuna, or soft herbs like mint, cilantro, parsley, or chives. Less than 6 hours of sun isn't usually enough solar energy for most plants that make sugar- or fat-rich seeds or fruit (like beans or tomatoes) in addition to growing and keeping their leaves alive. To help enrich biodiversity, you can grow shade-loving plants like wild garlic, mint, lemon balm, bee balm, and yarrow. You can also grow vinca flower, bellflower, balloon flower, bleeding heart ferns, and sedges, which, while not edible by humans, attract pollinators and create a habitat for insects, microbes, and even birds.

South

A southern exposure gives access to the most intense sunlight. A south-facing garden allows you to grow the greatest variety of plants, including those most hungry for light such as tomatoes, peppers, and most other fruiting plants.

However, if you live in an especially hot or dry climate, or if your growing space is surrounded by reflective or radiant surfaces (like lots of glass or light-colored walls or concrete) you might need to do more to temper the abundant heat and glare that your setting provides. You can try growing heat- and drought-tolerant plants, adding shade cloths, and creating shade by growing sunflowers and sun-loving vining vegetables such as cucumber and pole beans. You can also mulch heavily to preserve water in the soil. If you still struggle to grow vegetables in the summer, you may need to focus most of your growing efforts on autumn, spring, or even winter.

East and West

Between the extremes of northern and southern exposures, eastern and western exposures offer a medium amount of light, conducive to growing many types of plants, though western exposures tend to get warmer, since they receive their strongest light later in the day when heat has built up.

WIND

If you're gardening on a balcony, you'll also be more exposed to the effects of wind. Wind is above all a safety consideration when thinking about containers on a balcony, and securing all containers, especially smaller ones, is vital. Regularly check the fastenings and supports for any window boxes, and consider bringing window boxes and small pots inside before big storms.

After safety considerations have been addressed, remember that wind is drying to all plants, but especially those in containers. And don't forget windchill: Winds in cold weather can intensify the damaging effects of the cold, so your wind-blown balcony plants may be more affected by windchill than more-sheltered plants at street level.

Sunset on my southwestern-facing balcony vegetable garden

SETTING UP YOUR CONTAINER GARDEN

SIZE

Define how much of your given space you want to dedicate to your container garden. It helps to sketch the layout, including the entrance and exit to the area, how you will move around the garden space, what space you need to save for other activities like parking the car if your garden is by the driveway, and where you will place the containers. Keep in mind that your plants will grow beyond the bounds of your containers. It is essential for you to be able to move easily around them to care for, water, and harvest them.

Research the full-grown size of the plants you want to grow. However you choose to lay out your space, keep in mind the permaculture principle to "start small." Even if you have lots of room, I recommend you start with only a few containers, then gradually add to the garden. This will give you the chance to get the hang of it without the expense or frustration that can be overwhelming.

View of my garden in early October, taken from my neighbor's balcony

Cultivated arugula, winter lettuce, and lamb's lettuce in mid-January

CONTAINERS

Among the containers available on the market from secondhand and thrift stores or even trash picking, there are four main types.

Geotextiles (Synthetic Cloth)

Planters made from woven synthetic fabrics are increasingly available, with many options on the market. They are generally rot-proof, weather and UV proof, and have the advantage of being easy to store after they've been used. Best of all, especially for balcony gardeners and gardeners with mobility issues, they are incredibly lightweight.

Terra-Cotta

This material has the advantage of being all-natural and porous, allowing air and water to circulate as long as the pots aren't glazed. Terra-cotta containers dry quickly and remoisturize easily. What's more, you can find some with pretty designs that add to the aesthetic of your garden. As they're heavy, terra-cotta containers offer a certain amount of stability, but they're sensitive to shocks and frost, which makes them a little delicate and not the best choice if they have to remain outside during winters experiencing days of below-freezing temperatures.

Especially on a balcony, or if you have mobility concerns, be aware that once you've filled the pots with soil, especially wet soil, they become very heavy.

Wood

Wood is pleasing to look at and is a renewable and biodegradable resource. I prefer containers made of non-treated wood that is naturally rot-resistant, such as black locust, chestnut, cedar, or oak. You can also make your own wooden containers out of wood pallets stamped "HT." These have been heat-treated to rid them of pathogens.

Plastic

This material is light, easy to handle, cheap, and relatively durable. On the flip side, plastic requires the combustion of fossil fuels to be made, making it a less sustainable material than wood or terra-cotta.

Alternative Containers

You can also plant in repurposed bird cages, wine crates, soil bags, plastic water jugs, and more. All you need to do is make holes through the bottom of the container for drainage. You can line especially porous containers with geotextile felt or a burlap bag to keep soil from washing out.

Size and Placement

The size of the containers you use will change according to the types of plants you select and how much space they need to grow and develop their roots. For example, the pots I own vary in depth from 6 to 20 inches (15 to 51 cm). In the smaller 6-inch-deep (15 cm) containers, I grow radishes, lettuce, arugula, and mâche. In the 12- to 20-inch (30 to 51 cm) pots, I grow tomatoes, eggplant, cucumber, climbing beans, and giant sunflowers, among other plants.

Keep in mind that rectangular containers are easier to fit together in small areas and will therefore

save space. Also, the larger your containers are, the better they'll conserve moisture and protect plants' roots from temperature shocks. On the other hand, they're more difficult to move around than smaller containers. When choosing container size, take all your factors into account and choose the largest containers possible given your budget, physical abilities, and the amount of time you're likely to be able to garden in that particular location.

As for me, I have both rectangular bins and window boxes as well as round terra-cotta pots gifted to me by friends, found in the garbage, and in some cases, bought at flea markets. This allows me to give containers a second life while saving money.

SAFETY

Safety is a special consideration if you're gardening on a balcony. You can ask your co-op board or building superintendent or manager to check how much weight your balcony can support. Once a container is filled with soil, especially wet soil, it can become extremely heavy. That's why I recommend you check each container's weight before purchasing and use well-aerated soil, which you can lighten by adding extra perlite (a mineral that constitutes the white flecks in most commercial potting soils). I prefer to hang window boxes on the inside of the railing or on solid supports. Finally, be mindful of how waterproof your balcony is, and be sure it drains in a way that won't bother your downstairs neighbors or damage the building.

TOOLS

While you might not need a full-size shovel, to grow a container garden you'll still need some tools. Here are some of the tools I use all the time.

1. Gloves
2. Clippers
3. A pair of scissors
4. A hand trowel
5. A hand cultivator
6. Plant markers
7. A pencil and eraser
8. A progress notebook
9. Intermediate transplant pots
10. A dibbler
11. A handheld seeder
12. Some string for attaching plants to stakes or teepees

A seedling tray
A watering can
One or two mini greenhouses
A sifter
A harvest basket
One or more protective plant covers (like horticultural fleece) to extend the planting season and/or protect the vegetable garden during sudden frosts

Don't hesitate to adopt a "found object" frame of mind! Even broken objects can be repurposed. For example, I sometimes fished paper drinking cups out of the garbage at my workplace and brought them home to use for transplanting tomato seedlings.

Everyday Objects That Can Be Used as Container Gardening Tools

TOOL	SUBSTITUTE
Hand trowel	Large soup spoon
Hand cultivator	Fork
Plant markers	Pieces of a wooden crate or cut up plastic milk jugs (write on them with a Sharpie)
Watering can	Plastic bottle or jug with a punctured lid
Seedling tray	Toilet paper rolls or paper towel rolls cut in half
Seed spreader	A semi-rigid piece of paper measuring 4 to 5 inches by 2.5 to 3 inches (10 to 13 cm by 6.5 to 7.5 cm), folded in half
Mini greenhouse	Clear plastic bottle or tub with a capacity of a gallon or more
Sifter	Sieve
Harvest basket	Salad bowl, large plate, or tray
Intermediate transplant pots	Take-out containers with holes punched in them

This is a non-exhaustive list! You'll probably come up with some great ideas of your own.

SOIL

While almost every new garden's soil needs work, this is especially obvious to the new container gardener, who has to bring in *all* their new soil. The quality and price of soil can vary greatly. I use an all-purpose potting soil that says "Certified Organic" on the label. Multifunctional soils can be used for germinating seeds, transplanting seedlings, and for planting directly in containers.

Sifting soil to remove its coarse components

The longer you have your garden, the more of its own materials (leaves, stems, dead flowers, and so on) you can recycle back into it to make more soil over time. This process is known as composting. (Learn more about this on page 72.)

When I'm germinating seeds, especially delicate seeds such as lettuce, celery, or parsley, I sift the soil to obtain a density comparable to what is sold commercially as "seed starting mix," free of large fibers or clumps that could inhibit the seeds' sprouting. Sometimes I sift worm compost obtained from my worm compost bin or from friends who compost but have more than they need, or from a neighborhood exchange (see page 73 for more about worm composting). I also reuse soil from plants that no longer produce, as long as they weren't diseased. I crumble the soil (preferably when dry) and remove all the root clusters before I sieve it. Keep in mind that new nutrients (such as from compost) will need to be added to this soil.

PREPARING YOUR CONTAINERS

Before I prepare my containers, I make sure they are clean and have good drainage so water doesn't remain in the container and stagnate, which can stress plants' roots and encourage infections and rot.

I cover the bottom in a 1.25- to 4-inch (3 to 10 cm) layer of clay pebbles depending on the size of the container. I add a layer of geotextile fabric on top of the pebbles—an optional step that helps keep the soil and pebbles separate, for easier transplanting later—and then fill the container with soil up to 1.25 inches (3 cm) below the top rim. If I don't have any clay pebbles, I use broken terra-cotta pots, found tiles, or cracked dishes that I break up into smaller pieces. You can find amazing things on a bulk waste day or on free giveaway websites such as freecycle.org or buynothingproject.org.

Sometimes I use broken shards of old pots in place of clay pebbles.

SOW SEEDS OR BUY PLANTS?

In my own garden, I choose to grow plants from seeds, either by sowing them directly in containers outside or by starting them indoors in seedling trays before transplanting them outside. But depending on how much time you have, your budget, and the time of year you begin your container garden, you might prefer to buy your plants. If you don't have much free time to devote to germinating seedlings, then just buy them: You'll be able to establish your garden faster.

It's worth noting, however, that when buying seedlings, you won't have the same diversity of choice you would if you were to grow your own from seeds. You can find a wider variety of seedlings if you seek out an organic farm or specialist nursery that stocks a greater selection of vegetable plants. Keep in mind, however, that these come with a heftier price tag. In the spring, you may be able to get hold of interesting free plants by trading with other amateur gardeners.

In general, you'll find more choice of plants at garden centers, plant sales, and farmers markets, and from organic commercial growers, in the spring than in the fall. If you wait until the end of the summer, there'll be much less—if anything—on offer. At that point, you'll have to resort to working with seeds if you wish to grow (and your climate allows for) a fall-winter garden.

I favor diversity and remain in awe of watching the magic of a seed germinate, so I always grow my own plants.

'Miniature Navy' beans germinating

*Japanese mustard, also
called 'Purple Mizuna,'
seedlings grown in a tray
of aerated soil*

Growing Plants from Seeds

I like to grow my own plants so that I have access to varieties that are infrequently, if ever, available on the market ready-grown. For example, as a tomato lover, I have more varieties of tomatoes to choose from in seed packets than as commercially grown seedlings. What's more, growing my own plants is very economical, because the cost of a whole packet of seeds is considerably cheaper than buying a few established plants. The quantity of seeds in a package gives you the opportunity to grow several seeds at once, save some for the next year, give some away, or trade them with other gardeners.

Finally, please be aware that some vegetable garden plants are not offered for sale as seedlings, such as carrots, peas, and beans. You'll have to plant the seeds either in a small pot, or directly into the soil.

Growing your own plants, especially from seeds, requires a bit of organization because you have to take into account the pace at which the seedlings develop, as well as their needs, and of course plan the right time to plant them. For example, I sow peppers and eggplant indoors as early as February, as they take a long time to grow, and tomatoes in staggered plantings from early February to the beginning of April. The idea is that, when started early, the seedlings will be sufficiently developed before they are transplanted into their permanent placement, usually in May, once the soil has warmed up and there is no danger of frost. My February sowings also allow me to have plants ready for the first plant exchanges in the springtime.

Bell pepper seedlings

Growing Plants from Tubers and Bulbs

I grow some vegetables, such as potatoes and onions, from tubers or bulbs that I buy from an organic food market, where they are grown without any hormone treatment that slows their sprouting. You can also do this with sweet potatoes, heads of garlic (using their outer cloves), or scallions. Of course, you can also find seeds and "starts" for potatoes, garlic, shallots, and onions (often called "sets") from good seed companies.

Germinated 'Bleu d'Artois' potatoes

SEED ANCESTRY

There are two main kinds of seeds available to home growers: F1 hybrids and open-pollinated seeds.

F1 hybrids, which stands for "Filial 1," are the first generation of a cross between two distinct varieties of plants, usually within the same species or sometimes across closely related species. All the plants produced within one hybrid F1 generation will be uniform in appearance in terms of size and color, or will have specific aptitudes, like resistance to shock during transport or handling. But plants grown from seeds saved from an F1 plant won't resemble their F1 parents exactly because certain traits reappear randomly in the offspring. Therefore, it is not advised to save and plant seeds gathered from a hybrid plant.

Conversely, open-pollinated seeds descend from the same cultivar, or variety, for many generations. They have genetic diversity from generations of different parent plants, but their key characteristics come back dependably from seed throughout the generations. To give a parallel example from the animal kingdom, when Goldendoodle dogs were first introduced, most had parents that consisted of a purebred poodle and a purebred golden retriever, making them F1 hybrids. But as Goldendoodles grew in popularity and their population grew, it became viable to breed two Goldendoodle parents, rather than always mating a poodle with a golden retriever. The more generations of Goldendoodles that descend from Goldendoodle parents and grandparents, the more distinct and stable the Goldendoodle variety becomes, as with open-pollinated seeds.

The diverse genetic ancestry of open-pollinated seed varieties makes them more adaptable to different regions, to the effects of climate change, and to our various gardening practices. If you want to reduce the waste of packaging and shipping, share abundance with neighbors, and be certain of what will grow from the seeds you save, it's best to buy seeds that specify they're "open-pollinated." By doing this and then saving seed from your plants, you can buy one packet of a certain kind of tomato seeds and grow that variety for years to come. Harvesting seeds from my plants is one of my favorite pastimes; I explain how to do so on page 90.

'Daylight White' scabiosa seeds

In Europe, open-pollinated seeds are often referred to as "peasant seeds." In the French documentary *Seed Tour*, Véronique Chable, a research engineer at the National Institute for Agricultural Research (Institut National de la Recherche Agronomique/INRA), defined peasant seeds as: "A farm-raised seed, grown in the terroir, and maintained by farmers in coevolution with the terroir, climate, humans, and the prevailing culture. It's based solely on natural processes, on diversity, and reproduced at the farm, free of copyright, tradeable."

Preserving Variety

As an ambassador of the civilian movement Graines de Vie, or "seeds of life," which aims to preserve diversity in vegetable and fruit varieties at risk of extinction in the Paris region, I garden with only open-pollinated seeds to help preserve variety, to adapt and reproduce them.

According to a 2010 report of the UN FAO (Food and Agriculture Organization), 75 percent of fruit, vegetable, and cereal varieties have disappeared over the past 100 years due to the homogenization of crops. Besides advocating for the preservation of variety in general, I also support the artisan seed collectives and organizations fully dedicated to the preservation of heirloom varieties. Reproducing my own seeds allows me to save money—nature is that generous. And this way, I can also share or trade them with other amateur gardeners.

Where to Find Seeds

You'll have no problem finding seeds and plants in specialized locations such as nurseries and home improvement stores, but many will be F1 varieties. Open-pollinated seeds are available on the websites of artisan farmers, collectives, and associations for the preservation of cultivated biodiversity such as Seed Savers Exchange. Organizations like Native Seed/SEARCH, Southern Exposure Seed Exchange, North Circle Seeds, and others specialize in heirloom, open-pollinated seeds uniquely suited to unique regional climates, such as the Southwest, the Upper Midwest, the Southeast, and more.

Organic Seeds

Seed packages marked "certified organic" simply mean that they were produced in keeping with the specifications of organic agriculture. You can find it just as often on packages of F1 hybrids as open-pollinated seeds.

SOWING SEEDS

Sowing consists of putting seeds in the ground, whether in a small pot or directly into the permanent growing container, and then giving them the moisture and temperature conditions they need to grow. These are the three ways to sow seeds.

White chard seeds in rows

- **In a row:** I trace a groove (also known as a furrow) into which I place the seeds in a single row, either by hand or using a seeder. This is the best method for small seeds like lettuce. Always read the seed packet to find out the best depth and spacing for the seeds you're planting. Usually, the smaller the seed, the shallower the planting.

'Coco de la Meuse' bean seeds in holes

- **In a small hole:** I make a hole in the soil into which I place a few seeds.

- **Randomly:** I scatter the seeds evenly in a small pot or container.

Large seeds, such as beans, lend themselves better to planting in rows or in pockets. For zucchini seeds, I drop one seed into each small pot, because once they germinate, the seedlings grow quickly and take up all the space.

Seeds randomly scattered for the cutting lettuce 'Blushed Butter Oak'

When to Sow

Every variety of garden vegetable has its own timeline and specific temperature range for best germination and growth. Some plants, like radishes, are ready to harvest quickly, don't need lots of heat and light, and can be successfully planted almost anytime. Others, like peppers and squash, need long weeks of summer heat and light to grow to maturity. You can usually find this information on the back of the seed package. Nevertheless, I also rely on planting calendars available online and use this information to make my own calendar, which I refine to match my variety of plants and geographical zone. Calendars give average indications, but depending on weather patterns, you may want to plant a little earlier or later in the season from one year to the next.

Besides planting calendars, I carefully observe my environment and take cues from the indicators that nature provides in zones beyond my container garden. For example, I've learned that the springtime flowering of forsythia in my apartment complex's courtyard tells me that I can sow my leafy greens and peas, and when the lilacs bud in my neighborhood, it's time to plant the potatoes. When my neighbor's roses bloom, I know to transplant the tomatoes, peppers, eggplant, zucchini, and cucumber into their final locations.

Finally, I stay attentive to my local climatic conditions to move up or delay certain sowings and/or transplantings.

Vegetable Germination Temperatures

AROUND 45 TO 46°F (7 TO 8°C)	ABOVE 50°F (10°C)	ABOVE 59°F (15°C)	ABOVE 68°F (20°C)
Carrot	Beet	Basil	Eggplant
Lettuce	Cabbage	Bell pepper	
Lima beans	Leek	Celery	
Radish	Onion	Chicory and endive	
Spinach	Parsley	Chile pepper	
	Swiss chard	Chives	
	Turnip	Cilantro	
		Cucumber	
		Orach	
		Squash	
		Tomato	
		Zucchini	

'Mrs. Burns'' lemon basil seedlings

Soaking bean seeds before sowing

For example, in 2019 to 2020, we had a particularly mild winter and a relatively warm and early spring in the Paris region. I decided to transplant a few 'Red Robin' cherry tomato plants onto my balcony early on April 1 and then again on April 15 when I would usually do this in May. Nonetheless, I kept the majority of my tomato varieties inside to transplant in mid-May. Late frosts can wreak havoc on your garden if you plant out too soon.

Of course, there are other markers of the growing season, many unique to your local environment. Getting to know the seasonal markers around you is one of the joys of gardening!

Soaking Seeds

Most large or hard seeds appreciate being soaked for 6 to 12 hours before being put in the soil. Be careful not to let them soak for more than 24 hours to prevent them from rotting once in the soil. After experiencing this firsthand, I now only soak bean seeds for 12 hours.

Soaking seeds jump-starts the germination process. On a practical level, it's easier to sow larger seeds that have soaked than smaller seeds. Little seeds such as parsley will cluster. As a rule, I soak green bean, pea, fava bean, and sometimes cucumber, zucchini, and squash seeds. Soaking them also

makes them easier to sort through. Fertile seeds tend to sink, and the non-viable ones float on the surface of the water. If there are seeds still floating after several hours, compost them and plant the good seeds.

(1) 'Coco de la Meuse'; (2) 'Borlotto' (staked); (3) 'Goldfield'; (4) 'Red Noodle'; (5) 'Beurre de l'Oncle Christian'; (6) 'Kilometer'; (7) 'Blauhilde'; (8) 'La Vigneronne'

How Deep to Sow

It's a question I asked myself often when I first began gardening, but there is a rule of thumb: Most seeds should be planted at a depth three times their width. Small seeds, like carrot seeds, can simply be deposited on the surface and lightly covered with sifted soil. Make a small mound over them so that after a light watering they will be in close contact with the damp soil.

Vegetable Sowing Depths

0.25 TO 0.5 INCH (0.5 TO 1.25 CM)	0.75 INCH (2 CM)	1.25 INCH (3 CM)
Arugula	Beet	Beans
Cape gooseberry	Cabbage	Corn
Carrot	Chard	Garlic
Chervil	Cilantro	Lima beans
Chicory and endive	Cucumber	Onion (bulbs)
Chile pepper	Mâche	Pea
Chinese chives	Orach	Shallot (bulbs)
Chives	Radish	Zucchini
Dill	Turnip	
Eggplant		
Leek		
Lettuce		
Parsley		
Pickling cucumber		
Sorrel and red-veined sorrel		
Tomato		

How to Sow

I prepare my seedling trays ahead of time—brushing them out; disinfecting them with white vinegar, which works just as well as using chemical disinfectants; and rinsing and drying them. I organize my seed packages, identification labels, and sifted soil. Uncleaned pots can carry diseases that will affect the seeds, so don't skimp on cleanliness. After disinfecting my seedling trays, I simply fill them with sifted soil up to a little less than 0.5 inches (1.25 cm) from the top, and then gently press it down with my fingers or the back of a spoon.

Label

I prepare a plant marker with the name of the variety and date and insert one into each small pot. I do this now (and not at the end) to avoid mislabeling my seeds. One trick is to use a pencil rather than a pen or permanent marker. Pencil lasts over time, doesn't run, and can later be erased and the marker/label put to new use.

Place the seeds in the furrow

To plant in rows, depending on the size of the container (small pot, tub, or tray), I begin by lightly tracing furrows up to 1 to 1.5 inches (3 to 4 cm) apart.

Then I drop the seeds into the grooves, either with my hands or with a seeder. I make sure to space the seeds apart to allow the seedlings to develop easily and limit stress during transplanting. As the French saying goes: "If you sow abundantly, you'll get little. If you sow little, you'll get abundance."

For larger seeds such as zucchini and legumes, I make small holes with my finger or a pencil. I drop the seeds in, then I cover with soil and pat down. I finish with a gentle watering.

For random planting, scatter the seeds sparingly over the surface of the soil, being mindful to space them out before scattering soil thinly over the top.

For peas and climbing green beans, I plant five seeds per small pot, all pressed into the soil with a fingertip to the appropriate depth.

Water

I cover the seeds with sifted soil (how much depends on the size of the seeds) and water very delicately, either with a mister, or dribbling with the help of my perforated water jug. Gentle watering means you won't risk displacing the seeds in the containers. Another way (my preferred way) consists of setting small pots and/or seed trays in another shallow container of water for several hours. This watering technique draws water gently up into the container through the drainage holes via capillary action. This method is more time-consuming but allows the soil to absorb as much water as it needs. However, be careful not to let the seed tray sit in water for too long once the surface is damp to the touch! Oversaturating seeds can lead to rot. The other advantage is that the water will slowly conform to the temperature of the soil, helping to avoid shocking seeds with cold water.

*Pocket climbing/staked green bean
seeds 'Blauhilde' and 'Goldfield'*

Tomato and bell pepper seedlings in a miniature greenhouse

Keeping the Seeds Warm

In temperate climates such as mine in Paris—and certainly in even colder climates—plants with longer life cycles whose seeds need warmth to germinate should be started early indoors in order to assure a harvest before the weather turns cold again. This is the case with tropical vegetables such as tomato, eggplant, bell pepper, chile pepper, and Cape gooseberry. As the season progresses, these plants will have a difficult time reaching maturity if the seed doesn't start in a warm environment in February or March. Starting your seeds inside gives them a head start.

Germination

To germinate, seeds need optimal moisture, warmth, and oxygen. What is optimal for one kind of seed might be negative for another, hence the importance of getting to know different seeds' needs. During germination, a seed's outer envelope softens and tears open, allowing roots to take hold, and then the stalk produces "seed leaves," or cotyledons. Following that, the first "true" leaves appear with characteristics common to each variety.

The great majority of seeds can germinate in the dark. Some, however, are photosensitive and need light to sprout. This is the case with arugula, for example, which I discovered when I imitated nature and sprinkled the seeds randomly right on top of soil without covering them. This is because plants, at the end of their vegetative cycle, go to seed and let their seeds fall to the ground, where they usually remain uncovered. After the first rain, if the conditions are right, the seeds will germinate.

Depending on which vegetable I have sown, especially when I'm raising seedlings for transplanting, I keep the vegetables that need warmth to germinate (tomatoes and peppers) indoors, especially overnight when temperatures drop. In the case of lettuce or orach, which can germinate in colder temperatures, I keep the containers outdoors.

As soon as plants germinate, I place the containers under a specialized grow-light or somewhere they'll get bright sunlight, in a room that's not too warm. If you put seedlings on a windowsill, be sure to turn them often so they get even sun exposure. This helps prevent them from becoming leggy, a term for when a stalk elongates in search of light in an overly warm environment. In addition, if you position your young seedlings outdoors on warm days, like I do, you might do well to cover them with netting to protect them from birds or rodents. Several times, I've caught pigeons in the act of digging up seedlings!

If Your Plants Become Leggy

Don't panic: You can try to compensate for the longer stem by digging seedlings up and, being careful not to break the stem, transplanting them at a greater depth. Cover more of the stem with soil but leave the cotyledons above the surface. This is most successful with tomato seedlings and may not always work, but it's worth a try.

'Gold Rush' zucchini seedling

TRANSPLANTING

Transplanting consists of removing a young plant from its small pot and replanting it in another larger container or its permanent placement. When you're working with multiple seedlings in one small container, you'll be able to tell when they start crowding each other. This means they should be planted in small pots of their own so that they have enough space and nourishment to grow. This is when I transplant the seedlings I've kept indoors such as tomatoes, chiles, bell peppers, eggplant, and Cape gooseberries, and those I germinated on the balcony (sometimes under an overhang for protection) such as lettuce, cabbage, and leeks.

When to Transplant

I transplant once the seedlings have developed at least two sets of true leaves, following the appearance of the cotyledons.

How to Transplant

Step 1

A few hours before transplanting, I water the plants. This helps loosen the soil around the roots and also hydrates the young plants before a stressful experience.

Step 2

From a seed tray
With the help of a fork or chopstick, I loosen the soil around the plant or plants as gently as possible, making sure not to damage the roots.

From a small flexible pot
I gently squeeze the pot a few times to help release the plant, making sure the roots are still surrounded by earth.

Root development of 'Blauhilde' pocket green bean seeds

Step 3

In a small pot
Touching only the leaves to avoid the delicate roots or stem, I place the seedling into a small pot containing a little earth at the bottom. I position the plant in the middle, then add soil all around the base of the stem and press down lightly.

In a permanent container
I dig a little hole and place the plant in it along with its root ball. I surround the stem with earth and then press down lightly with my hands.

Step 4

Water the plant in its new location gently but thoroughly.

Step 5

If I'm moving plants outside, I place the newly transplanted seedlings in a shady spot for a few days. Transplanting exerts some stress on plants. Placing them in the shade gives them the optimal place to recover and acclimate to life outdoors.

Transplanting with Bare Roots

Vegetables such as leeks and lettuce tolerate being transplanted with bare roots, without soil attached. When I transplant leeks, I sometimes trim back the roots and leaves, bringing them down by about a third of their total

Transplanting a bare-roots lettuce seedling

Bare-roots young lettuce plants

length from the root line to optimize their establishment. When I transplant lettuce, I cut away some of the loose leaves, leaving the crown and roots intact.

"Damping Off" in Seedlings

Damping off is a fungal disease that attacks seeds, causing them not to germinate, and young seedlings, which turn brown, droop, and then rot. The principal cause is excess humidity in the air or dampness in the soil because it allows fungus to grow in the seeds' outer shells or in the soil.

As a preventive measure, always buy good quality seeds and use fresh soil for germination, use clean containers washed with white vinegar, and make sure the soil is not packed too tightly and isn't kept soaking wet. Also, don't sow too densely and/or consider thinning, and finally, store the seeds in a place where the temperature remains constant. In very humid conditions, a small clip fan on a low setting pointed over seedlings can help prevent diseases that thrive in damp atmospheres.

A Garlic Infusion for Plant Health

To prevent damping off, one trick is to make a garlic infusion to spray on seedlings, as garlic has antifungal and insect-repellent properties.

Use the infusion as soon as it's ready because you can't preserve it. It also treats mildew and rust. Make sure your seeds are viable and fertile. Seeds have a variable germination period depending on the species and varieties. Seeds that aren't preserved in appropriate conditions may not germinate at all (see "Growing Plants from Seeds," page 38).

Garlic Infusion

I recommend spraying the insides of your flowerpots with this solution before filling them with soil as a preventive measure, or as soon as your seeds are affected by damping off. Use it sparingly, as you don't want to add to overly damp conditions that foster the same kind of pathogens you're trying to prevent!

——— MAKES 5 QUARTS (5 L) ———

8 to 12 garlic heads, cloves separated and peeled (about 500 g)
5 quarts (5 L) water

1. Roughly chop and soak the garlic in the water for 10 to 12 hours.
2. Bring the infused water (with the garlic still in it) to a boil and cook for 15 to 20 minutes.
3. Cool for around 10 hours, then strain. Use the infusion right away.

OTHER WAYS TO GROW YOUR OWN PLANTS

Cuttings

This way of reproducing plants consists of cutting off a piece of the mother plant and inducing it to grow its own roots, thus creating a new plant. Making cuttings is an easy technique for growing plants such as basil, mint, thyme, and even to my great surprise, Cape gooseberry (by cutting a hard, straight stem),

A strawberry plant grown by layering a parent plant's stolons

and tomato (by cutting a sucker, or a branch at the intersection of the main stalk and a leaf). I put the cuttings in water that I change regularly to prevent mold until I see the appearance and development of a good root system, then I plant them.

Layering

This technique consists of burying plant parts that characteristically develop roots even while they are still attached to the mother plant. For instance, strawberries grow stolons (a kind of root, also known as runners), at the end of which new small plants grow. I harvest these and either place them in water to develop their roots, or I transplant them into a small pot and water them.

Volunteer Seeds

Some plant varieties expel their seeds before I can harvest them (for example kale and borage). These seeds, which horticulturalists call "volunteers," sow themselves, and I can move the seedlings to wherever I want, which is an easy way to obtain new plants.

'Mandarin' pepper plant

'Grappe de Noël'

'Maïs Fraise' strawberry corn

'Mouchetée de Salasc' lettuce

'Westländer Winter' curly kale

'Mrs. Burns" lemon basil

In conclusion, growing your own plants has real advantages, such as:

- variety of choice
- savings compared to buying plants
- minimal use of soil, especially using growing trays
- ability to manage the seeds' environments (temperature, watering)
- availability of plants, in case the first batch dies off or is attacked by pests
- choice of where to transplant
- earlier harvest date as transplanted plants are well developed and shave one or two months off growing time
- ideal management of your crop

GETTING TO KNOW GROWTH CYCLES

Plants have different life cycles; the primary ones are as follows.

Perennials

These are plants that keep growing and producing for years at a time, like lovage, perennial cabbages and kale, strawberries, and dwarf fruit trees. Once planted, you can enjoy them for years! Perennials are a key part of many traditional permaculture designs because they reduce the energy needed to grow new plants every spring. They also allow more complex micro-ecosystems to develop around them over time.

Speckled romaine lettuce (an annual)

Annuals

These plants complete their life cycle within one year, from germination until they go to seed, the final stage of their lives. However, it's worth noting that some so-called annuals can have cycles that overlap two calendar years. For example, that's the case with winter lettuces in my mild temperate climate: Planted at the end of summer or in early fall and established before winter, they will only go to seed the next spring.

Strawberry (a perennial)

Biennials

Biennials such as beets go through the first part of their life cycle in the first year, developing roots, stems, and leaves. During the winter, they go dormant before finishing their cycle in the second year.

Cabbage (a biennial)

Indigo tomatoes grown from a volunteer seed

CHOOSING PLANTS WITH CONTAINERS IN MIND

Within each plant species, there are almost always certain cultivars, or varieties, that are more adaptable to container gardening. That's the case for 'Red Robin' tomatoes, a cherry tomato plant that grows to be about 12 inches (30 cm) tall and is perfectly happy in a window box or a pot 7 to 8 inches (18 to 20 cm) in diameter. As another example, the 'Slim Jim' eggplant is a compact plant with a relatively short growth cycle of around sixty days, making it an ideal addition to a container garden. Aside from size and growth speed, there are several other factors that make some cultivars either more or less suited for container gardens.

Annual Varieties

I choose annual plants mostly, so that I can benefit from quick and regular harvests, one after the other. However, I also grow some biennial plants such as kale, from which I can harvest a leaf at a time as early as the first year. Other biennial plants I grow include cabbage and broccoli, beginning in summer for a winter or spring harvest.

Fast-Growing and Early Varieties

These varieties are particularly useful in a small space as they have a short growth cycle, meaning they reach maturity before other varieties of the same species. 'Paris Market' cocktail carrots can be harvested three months after sowing. Another example is the 'Sub Arctic Plenty' tomato, which can be harvested one and a half to two months after transplanting.

'Red Ursa' curly kale

I also plant leafy greens and some root vegetables you can harvest when they are still young and then onward for the entire growth period. Because leafy greens grow outward, I harvest them by picking only the outside leaves (in order not to compromise their development) unless I need the space for another plant.

Perpetual Harvest

Other than chives, garlic chives, strawberries, and red sorrel, which can produce for several years in a vegetable garden, I don't grow any perennials for lack of space. But other gardeners with enough space and the right climate grow everything from apples to grapevines in containers!

First Harvest Timings

3 WEEKS AFTER PLANTING SEEDS	Early garden cress shoots, Persian cress, pea shoots and tendrils, and soft herbs such as chervil, cilantro, etc.
BETWEEN 1 AND 2 MONTHS AFTER PLANTING SEEDS	Young lettuce leaves, arugula, spinach, spring radishes, mibuna, green and purple mizuna, kale, scallions, and onions, including their edible green stalks.
BETWEEN 2 AND 3 MONTHS AFTER PLANTING SEEDS	Lettuce leaves or whole lettuce, Swiss chard, early broccoli varieties such as 'Calinaro' broccoli, dwarf beans, Chinese cabbage such as Napa and bok choy, and also herbs like parsley, chervil, cilantro, and sorrel, as well as fast-growing varieties of turnips, 'Paris Market' carrots, etc.
THREE MONTHS AFTER PLANTING SEEDS	Endive, escarole, mâche, fava beans, cucumber, fennel, baby potatoes, and short-season tomatoes.

Seeds and Staggered Planting

If you want to be able to harvest vegetables, herbs, or edible flowers throughout the season, you simply need to sow regularly. I plant only a small number of seeds at a time so that I can stretch my production and harvests throughout the year. For example, after I plant potatoes in March, I plant them again in July for a fall harvest. With zucchini and cucumber, I plant in April and again in June and July. For beans, I seed some in May and some in June and July.

Polyculture

Polyculture is in keeping with the permaculture ethic of favoring diversity and means simultaneously growing several varieties of plants together, no matter the size of the container. In general, when you observe natural environments, you can see polyculture at work. In every ecosystem, a great number of plant varieties cohabit in the same space, with just a few deserts being the exception. This diversity lends resilience you won't find in monoculture. With monoculture, if a harmful insect settles in, it's much more likely to reproduce and spread, no matter the vegetable. Conversely, in the case of polyculture, this same

Borage flowering: Its very short growth cycle allows me to harvest several times a season.

insect will be slowed down by the variety of species. I learned this lesson from observing nature and using and valuing diversity in my garden.

In general, I grow two to five different vegetable species together, whether in my window boxes or large containers. For example, I have three fennel plants, two lettuce, and one cilantro plant in the same window box—three different species. In another window box, I arranged chervil, a dwarf tomato

Polyculture of fennel, lettuce, and sulfur cosmos

In this window box, I've planted buckwheat, dahlias, flax (that has gone to seed), tomatoes, kale, and orach.

plant, an Indian carnation, lemon basil, and purple orach whose leaves I'll harvest just before the tomato needs more room to spread out. This technique allows me to optimize my harvest according to the vegetables' varying growth cycles and their root or aerial development, to pick small and diversified quantities at a time, and to have a resilient garden less vulnerable to pests. Plus, my creativity can have free reign: I can plant by themes such as color, plant origin, and so on.

Companion Planting

This is another technique found in nature and falls under the broader umbrella of polyculture. It means planting different species with mutual beneficial properties next to each other. Companion planting works by taking advantage of the biochemical secretions of one species, released at the root level, aboveground, or during decomposition, to aid in the germination, growth, or survival of another species. Companion planting can limit the presence of disease and pests, increase productivity, optimize the use of space in the vegetable garden by increasing the density of plants all year long, manage the timing of harvests, increase biodiversity, and overall, favor the garden's equilibrium.

Herbs can act as deterrents thanks to their strong odors, which disorient pests that rely on scent to find their host plant. As for legumes, their roots embed the essential nutrient nitrogen in your garden soil. And nasturtiums attract aphids, keeping them off other vegetable garden plants.

When I practice companion planting, I begin by selecting the main crop, or the plant with the longest growth cycle from planting to harvest, or that will take up the most room.

Then, I add beneficial secondary plants with the same growth cycle. If tomatoes are my main crop, then I'll plant basil, marigolds, and/or carrots as a secondary crop. If my container still has room, I add other plants that will optimally make use of the remaining growing space. For instance, I'll plant crops with short growth cycles, like radishes, and lettuce, or pole beans, which will use a tomato plant as a stake.

Finally, if the main crop can't grow well before the nights are warm in spring or once the temperature drops again in autumn, like tomato, I decide which plants I'm going to grow in the container before and after the main crop. In order to optimize the harvests, I favor plants with a short growth cycle, such as radish or lettuce, to fill the place that will later be occupied by the main plant.

Put simply: Grow as many varieties as you can in the least space.

A 'Red Ursa' kale, gone to seed, provides shade for a round cabbage.

Lemon basil at the foot of a tomato plant

Chervil and Japanese mustard 'Komatsuna'

'Red Metamorph' marigold at the foot of a tomato plant

Planting Crops Close Together

In order to produce more in a small space, I purposefully condense my crops as much as possible. According to the variety, I reduce the distance between plants a good third from what an in-ground gardener might, or even more. For example, for cut-and-come-again lettuces such as red salad bowl, green salad bowl, and radichetta, don't hesitate to plant close together, even if you have to thin the seedlings out in stages and harvest in small batches.

Climbing beans supported by stakes

There is, however, a limit to planting density, and it can cause disease due to the compromised air circulation between the plants, so experiment with caution.

A few plants that can be planted densely together are:

- lettuces and radishes
- carrots and radishes
- chard and mâche
- potatoes and green beans or peas

The Time-Space Continuum

In order to grow as many vegetables as possible, I garden in multiple dimensions: in time and space.

You can optimize time by growing plants that ripen at different times, and space by using bamboo structures (like trellises or teepees) that support the vertical growth of vegetables such as pole beans and climbing peas. I always sow peas and fava beans in the fall, in October or early November, as I've noticed that the plants have done well over the past five winters. I harvest them in early spring, just in time to cede the space to the tomatoes. While my longer growing season gives me more time to play with, almost every growing season, no matter the length, provides opportunities for staggered harvests.

Garden Year-Round

Many gardeners think of gardening in the fall and winter as pointless, when in fact many climates allow for plentiful harvests during these seasons. This is likely to be increasingly true given climate change, and in Hardiness Zones 8 and above, you might find fall and winter are the only times you can successfully grow cool-weather crops like cabbage, endive, beets, all-season lettuces and radishes, winter radishes, mâche, spinach, white onions, and Japanese mustards such as mizuna and mibuna.

I start sowing these fall and winter vegetables either before the summer harvest, if I have room in my garden, or just after, if I need to wait until the summer harvest frees up space in my garden.

In the winter, I make sure to use horticultural fleece. This kind of protective layer can increase the ambient temperature by several degrees, which makes all the difference. You can also use inverted clear plastic storage tubs to protect plants on cold nights—just be sure not to leave plants under them for days at a time, as they'll suffer from a lack of ventilation. And be sure to keep covers of any kind well-cleaned, as pathogens like fungal spores thrive in damp places.

FERTILE SOIL

Like all plants, vegetables need nutrients to grow. In containers, due to the limited amount of soil, these nutrients are quickly depleted and absolutely need to be renewed. I manage my garden's fertility in the following simple ways.

Surface Composting

I have manure worms in my containers, so the organic matter I place on the surface of the soil is broken down pretty quickly. If you get compost from a local source, it's likely you'll need to introduce invertebrates to your containers that will break down organic matter, even if you don't specifically introduce manure worms. You might just need to layer organic matter more thinly, since breakdown will be slower. Limiting surface compost to low-sugar waste helps keep animals from scavenging. Some examples of low-sugar organic waste include:

- garden waste such as weeds, leaves, and grass clippings (in limited amounts and as long as they haven't been sprayed with pesticides)
- newspaper, shredded paper, and small pieces of cardboard (but avoid glossy magazines)

- paper towels (as long as they haven't come into contact with household cleaners or chemicals)
- wilted greens and carrot tops
- clean eggshells
- used coffee grounds and filters and biodegradable tea bags

If you have space for a compost bin that's either covered or placed far enough away from your plants to prevent scavenging animals from digging or looking to your crops as an additional food source, you can compost a wider range of organic waste like fruit waste (including citrus in limited quantities) and even small amounts of old bread and grains.

Surface composting in one of my large growing containers: The Eisenia fetida *worms break down the vegetable waste.*

The "Lasagna" Method

Two years ago, I managed to make a "lasagna" in two of my large containers. Lasagna is another technique you can use to increase your soil's fertility and reduce the amount of new soil you have to buy commercially. To do this, alternate layers of carbonized matter (brown waste like chipped wood, dry leaves, shredded brown paper, and uncoated cardboard) and nitrogen waste (green or "wet" waste, like wilted leaves, or carrot or potato peels). I top that with a layer of soil or compost. To deter scavenging animals, you can even place a final layer of cardboard on top and cut holes to transplant seedlings through.

To get enough organic matter for my lasagnas, I collect vegetable waste from my neighborhood. In better weather, there are always plenty of organic waste bags left on the sidewalk the night before pick-up, along with cardboard boxes for recycling. I also collect unsold fruits and vegetables from organic shops if they can't be donated to a food bank. Once I've made my lasagnas, I immediately do my transplanting. This technique is incredibly effective as my plants flourish.

Worm Composting

In 2014, wanting to reduce waste, I began practicing worm composting. Here's how I set up my own homemade composter.

I started with two 2.5-gallon (10 L) plastic storage containers. I drilled several holes in the bottom and lid of one of these containers, leaving the second container intact. I stacked the container full of holes on top of the other container, added a mixture of shredded paper, cardboard cut into small pieces, organic waste (such as fruit and vegetable peels), and several of the *Eisenia fetida* worms to the top container, and then covered it with the pierced lid. The worms turned the contents into compost, and the bottom container caught the worm casting tea—a concentrated brown liquid formed from the earthworms' decomposition of organic matter, which is particularly rich in nutrients, minerals, and trace elements. (Despite its name, it is for plant consumption only!) I stored my composter under my kitchen sink, gradually adding more organic waste to the top container. (Once the top container is full of compost, you can add another pierced container on top for additional organic waste. The worms in the middle container will migrate to this new container in search of food.)

After a few misadventures in the summertime when I had a fruit fly problem, I moved my worm compost to the basement, where the temperature stays more consistent. I made worm tea for several years before stopping because it wasn't practical to have to go down to my building's basement all the time, so I started putting my kitchen waste in the city's community composting collection bins that I pass on my way to work.

In March 2020, during the COVID-19 lockdown, I went back to my own worm composting, as there were no community bins at that time. I collected a handful of worms from my growing containers to use in my worm compost. Very quickly, I was able to harvest some worm casting tea, which I dilute to the ratio of 0.25 gallons (1 L) of tea mixed with 2.25 gallons (9 L) of water and use to feed my garden as well as my indoor plants. As for the compost, you'll need to be patient—it takes around six months for the worms to break down the organic matter.

Earthworms in North America

Because of their efficiency at clearing through organic matter, earthworms can be a great boon to small-space composters. However, across much of North America, earthworms of almost every species were introduced from Europe and Asia and are invasive. While there are many responsible ways to practice worm composting in North America, if you plan to introduce worms directly into your larger containers or if your container garden is close to open soil or larger ecosystems like woods or parks, research what kind of worms you obtain and whether they've been found to be especially aggressive in your local ecosystem. The *Eisenia fetida* worms I use in my containers haven't proven to be overly aggressive in most colder environments as they can't survive bitterly cold winter temperatures, especially not in containers elevated above soil level.

Finding and Sharing Compost

In urban areas, more and more communities offer composting to reduce the amount of garbage created. Several communities, including mine, hand out free compost bins, worm composters, and compost collection-pails. In Paris, there are collection bins for kitchen waste in almost every neighborhood.

Often city-dwellers who compost or make worm casting tea find themselves with a lot more than they need and don't know what to do with it. The co-op council members believe in composting, and always invite me to their "composting cocktail parties" at a nearby residential building. I have a good time and get to go home with some sieved compost. And finally, I belong to a neighborhood exchange and can sometimes get compost by posting a message online.

When I can't find enough compost to meet my needs, I buy it online. This year, I planted vegetables like zucchini which have a greater need for fertilizer, so I bought worm compost and horse manure suitable for organic farming.

Liquid Plant Fertilizers

Some natural liquid fertilizers derived from nettle and comfrey are useful and very affordable. These two fermented extracts have an abundance of benefits to encourage growth. Nettle (*Urtica dioica*) contains nitrogen for foliage growth, and the potassium in comfrey (*Symphytum officinale*) aids to encourage the growth of flowers and fruits.

If you find a place to forage nettles and comfrey (such as an empty lot or a friend's yard) you can make liquid fertilizer even in the city.

In the spring, I don my gloves to harvest nettle before it goes to flower. I cut it up and mix around 2 pounds (1 kg) of fresh nettles with 2 to 3 gallons (10 L) of water in a plastic bucket (not metal, which will oxidize) and cover it. I let it ferment for around two weeks, stirring the mixture once a day until there are no more bubbles on the surface. Then I dilute the mixture by 10 percent and use it to water my plants. Note that the fermentation of liquid fertilizer produces a very unpleasant smell! This is why I usually prepare it in my community garden plot rather than on my balcony. I make nettle manure every year and comfrey manure more rarely, as there aren't very many places in the city where I can harvest comfrey.

WATER

Water is one of the precious resources that a permaculture design approach seeks to conserve and channel in beneficial ways. Unlike growing in the ground where plants can send roots deep down in search of water, containers limit this survival technique. To limit the amount I have to water, I use large containers that are around 15 to 20 inches (38 to 51 cm) deep. I also use straw mulching and capillary watering (see "An Ancient Irrigation Technique: The Olla" on page 79), which preserve moisture. In the case of my small window boxes, whose earth dries very rapidly, I sometimes need to water every day.

Gardeners with an outdoor source of water have the advantage of being able to install a drip irrigation system. As I don't have a faucet outside, I use the following techniques.

Capturing Rain

My balcony has the advantage of being open to the elements, so when it rains my crops get watered. I always leave a few containers out to catch the rainwater. When evaluating the zones and sectors of your space (see pages 14–17), pay close attention to rainfall patterns and position thirsty plants and rainwater collection containers accordingly.

Hand Watering

Depending on weather conditions, evening is my preferred time to take my trusty watering can, filled from the kitchen sink, out to the balcony. Plants should be watered as deeply as possible, keeping in mind the current temperatures and wind conditions they're coping with. Manual watering is easily manageable for me due to the small size of my vegetable garden.

Planting Densely

Planting crops close together, especially alongside ground covers such as lettuce, helps keep water from evaporating and hence, slows containers from drying out. (See page 70 for more on this.)

Mulching and Surface Composting

You can also insulate soil from evaporation with plant detritus, like fallen or pruned leaves (making sure the leaves aren't diseased). This limits evaporation, preserves humidity, protects from erosion, and of course, reduces the amount of watering needed.

With limited space for a compost bin, I compost directly around my plants, and in addition to garden waste, I add some of the organic waste from my kitchen. This organic matter feeds the *Eisenia fetida* worms that I added to some of my containers. By breaking down plant detritus and kitchen waste, my little worms enrich the earth. (More on this subject under "Fertile Soil" on page 72.)

An Ancient Irrigation Technique: The Olla

This is an ancient technique of underground watering by capillary action that uses an irrigation jar called an olla (pronounced OH-ya). A terra-cotta pot is buried in the soil, leaving just the mouth exposed, and then filled with water. The mouth is then covered with a small terra-cotta saucer or lid to avoid evaporation. The porous nature of the terra-cotta allows water to seep slowly into the soil, watering the vegetables planted nearby.

*A hoverfly headed for a
'Sulfur Cosmos' flower*

WELCOME BIODIVERSITY

The first two fundamental ethics of permaculture instruct us to care for the earth and humans, in other words, all life-forms, as they are interdependent. At a time when biodiversity is severely threatened, and we're witnessing the disappearance of insect and bird populations in the countryside as well as in the city, growing a container garden is a chance to contribute in your own way, and to strive for the preservation of life in all its diversity, including plants as well as animals.

And in order for your vegetable garden to offer up its very best, there is nothing better than organic gardening without synthetic pesticides or chemicals. (The possession and use of these have been banned in France since 2019.) You can take it one step further and choose to actively foster biodiversity.

Insects are undeniably a key to gardening. Some insects, like bees and bumblebees, pollinate plants by transporting pollen from the male reproductive organ (the stamen) toward the female reproductive organs (the pistil), making possible fruits like zucchini, cucumber, and strawberries, while other insects such as ladybugs and their larvae efficiently regulate aphids. A ladybug on her own eats anywhere from 50 to 100 aphids a day, while its larvae can feast on around 150. To encourage these precious allies, here are some ways to welcome them into your garden by offering them room and board.

Diverse Vegetable Plants

I diversify my production, cultivating different varieties of vegetables, flowers, and herbs to attract as many beneficial insects as possible. I find

Bee foraging on a dahlia

Fly on a Japanese mustard leaf 'Osaka Purple'

Ladybug larva devouring an aphid

Ladybug on a lettuce plant

that planting open-pollinated seeds and heirloom plant varieties helps me achieve this variety.

Plants for Pollinators

Some plants are particularly good at producing pollen or nectar in large quantities. Nectar and pollen are the two main sources of nutrition for pollinator insects. I gladly include the following plants in my garden, especially for what their flowers offer bees, moths, butterflies, hoverflies, and other pollinators.

Vegetables
Zucchini, cucumber, fennel

Herbs
Cilantro, hyssop, basil, giant hyssop, chive, thyme

Flowers
Gaillardia, lupin, love-in-a-mist, Jack-in-the-bush, borage, calendula, cosmos, dahlia, sunflower, pincushion flower

Cover Crops
Lacy phacelia, buckwheat, wheat grass (see "Cover Crops" on page 84)

Morning Glory 'Carnevale di Venezia'

Basil 'Aromatto'

Other than vegetables such as zucchini, whose flowering is essential for it to be fruitful, I let herbs like cilantro go to seed. I also allow some leaf and root vegetables go to seed, so I can save the seeds for future plantings and provide food for pollinators. In early 2020, I planted kale and celery whose February–March blooming attracted many insects at a time of year when few flowers remain for gathering pollen or nectar. I make sure to stagger my flowering plants, so they'll bloom well into the fall.

Pests, Parasites, and Predators

A vegetable garden is an ecosystem inhabited by living organisms whose balance sometimes hangs by a thread. If this balance gets thrown off by the arrival of pests and parasites, predators are usually not far behind, drawn by the abundant source of food.

Following the permaculture principle to "observe and interact," and "self-regulate and accept negative feedback," and most of all, in order to garden *with* nature and not against it, I avoid interfering with pesticides and let the vegetable garden self-regulate.

For example, in spring 2020, I had to deal with a massive invasion of black aphids on vegetables of the Alliaceae family (chives, leeks), then green aphids on the Apiaceae (celery, parsley), and finally rosy apple aphids on the Brassicaceae (formerly Cruciferae, including kale and cabbage). The situation became so bad that I was overwhelmed. However, I sat tight, and luckily, one month after the aphids arrived, I saw, to my delight, the first ladybugs, then their eggs and larvae. Quite rapidly, the ladybugs and larvae began devouring the aphids, effectively regulating their population.

Cover Crops

If you have a very small container garden with just a few pots, you're unlikely to have containers sitting empty for any part of the growing season. However, if you have many containers—and maybe even a small raised bed or two—you might sometimes find yourself between plantings. Keeping seed for a quick-growing cover crop like buckwheat, wheat grass, or phacelia can be a way to crowd out weeds and provide food and shelter for wildlife until you're ready to grow vegetables in your garden again. These crops are also sometimes called "green manure" because when you're ready to plant a crop again, you can just turn the cover crop plants under the soil, cover with a little mulch, and plant straight into it (à la the "lasagna" method explained on page 73). The cover crop plants will decompose into the soil, returning its nutrients and fertilizing your future crops.

Stink bug eggs on the back of a tomato leaf

Leafminer in a 'Red Noodle' bean leaf

Green caterpillar on the back of a
'Coco de la Meuse' bean leaf

Aphids on a 'Red Ursa' kale seedpod

Other pests invaded the garden's periphery, such as the citrus leaf miner, insect larvae that look like tiny caterpillars, that munched holes in the green bean leaves, spinach, and chard. To solve the problem, I simply removed the affected leaves. At the base of borage leaves, I witnessed aphids being farmed by ants. The aphids, feeding on the sugar-rich sap, excrete honeyed translucent liquid that ants love. The ants protect the aphids from ladybugs, syrphid flies (aka flower flies or hover flies), and their larvae, to continue to benefit from the honeyed substance. I'd seen ladybug larvae around the garden, but not in that area. All of this burgeoning life helps keep the vegetable garden balanced.

In colder environments, shelter can be crucial for insects' winter survival. As a bonus, encouraging beneficial insects to hibernate in your garden means they'll be on hand first thing in spring. You can provide winter shelter for insects by leaving dead foliage in place until most of the spring frosts have passed.

'Purple Mizuna' before and after being visited by pigeons

Even a window box can shelter ladybugs and other hibernating insects like mason bees if you fill it with dead leaves, twigs, or small pieces of wood. Dried sunflower stalks are especially good shelter as they hollow with age.

Birds

My balcony garden is a mini oasis for city birds, as it offers them vegetation as well as food. I am delighted to be visited by tits, sparrows, and pigeons. Insect-eating birds are also a wonderful way of keeping caterpillar populations under control.

Overall, small birds don't do much damage and content themselves with pecking at certain leafy greens. But when I don't set out a bowl of water, the pigeons nibble on vegetables from the Brassicaceae family, such as arugula, purple mizuna, cabbage leaves, and broccoli heads. I had to relent and let the birds pick at the entirety of the black Tuscan cabbage. As for the broccoli, hoping there would be some left to eat, I covered its flowers with a cold weather covering. Finally, I also grow cosmos and sunflowers; their flowers delight both me and pollinators, and their seeds nourish the birds. To help the birds get through the winter, I provide suet until March. When spring comes, the birds are capable of finding their own food.

*Flowering kale
with seedpods*

SAVE YOUR SEEDS

It is relatively easy for an amateur gardener to produce their own seeds for future planting. All you need to do is select a certain number of plants known as seed carriers that will complete the germination cycle. Keep in mind that when some plants complete their growing cycle, they can take over some of the space in your garden. I'm thinking of broccoli, which has huge seed heads.

When garden space is limited, you might want to focus on plants that take up little room when they go to seed, such as spinach, kale, and lettuce, and especially seed and fruit vegetables such as green beans, peas, tomatoes, peppers, and so on.

How Seeds Are Made

Autogamy and Allogamy

These two concepts are essential in seed reproduction. Vegetable plants have two ways of reproducing themselves (although I'm not counting apogamy—asexual reproduction without fertilization).

- **Autogamous plants** are capable of self-fertilizing seeds within a single flower because it contains both the male and female organs. The flower's pollen will fertilize its own pistil. That's the case with green beans, peas, tomatoes, and lettuces.

- **Allogamous plants** are fertilized by the pollen of another flower, whether from the same plant or a different one. Zucchini, for example, produces separate female and male flowers. In order for a zucchini to develop, the female flower must be fertilized by the pollen of the male flower carried by pollinator insects.

Chervil seeds

Hybrids

It's common to see hybridization between two varieties of the same species, but it's easier to reproduce one variety per species, therefore avoiding hybridization—especially if you are a gardening beginner—and sticking to self-pollinating plants

How to Make Your Own Seeds

1. Identify the seed-producing plant

Begin by identifying and selecting one or several plants that you know grew from open-pollinated seeds to be your seed producer (see page 40 for more on why this is important). Choose plants with the best physical characteristics and attributes (a plant that developed well, was resistant to pests, or even was the tastiest). The selection can be made according to one or several criteria. In order to guarantee a certain degree of genetic diversity, I recommend having several seed-producing plants per species. This can be difficult to do in a container garden, since plants that are allowed to go to seed often take up a lot of space and must remain in the container for longer. To compensate for this, I recommend harvesting seeds from just one or two plants and, to introduce genetic variety, trading some of those seeds with other gardeners for seeds of the same variety from their own gardens.

2. Wait for the flowers

Grow the plants you've selected until they flower.

3. Leave some fruit

Let the flowering continue until it ends with the production of fruit containing the seeds (the pods of beans, peas, cabbage, and radishes, and fruit in the case of tomatoes or peppers).

4. Keep a close watch on the fruits

Let the fruits reach maturity and dry in the case of pods. Pay especially close attention to the ripening of seedpods for radishes and vegetables of the Brassicaceae family because, unlike pea or bean pods, once dry, they open and fling their seeds far and wide. For lettuces that flower from stalks carrying a multitude of little flowers at different stages of development, wait until the flowering is 75 percent complete. As for fruits derived from vegetable plants, pick at maturity or even when overripe.

5. Harvest

Harvest the seeds after a few dry weather days to have as little residual humidity as possible, which can contribute to rot, especially for seeds in pods or seeds from vegetables in the Aster family (lettuce).

6. Dry

Remove the seeds from their stalks or pods and let them dry. For watery fruit like tomato, either spread the pulp on a paper towel and let dry or proceed by fermentation. To do this, remove the pulp along with the seeds and place in a container such as a glass. Add a small amount of water and leave to ferment. After a few days, a white mold will develop on the surface. Pass the contents of the glass through a fine sieve and rinse with water. Drain and place the seeds on a plate, making sure to spread the seeds out, until completely dry.

'Glass Gem' corn

How to choose a storage container
Keep dry seeds in containers that can breathe, such as envelopes, paper bags, or jars with perforated lids. Be sure to mark the container with the variety, date, and place where you harvested the seeds. If you live in an especially humid environment, you might need to place seed envelopes in sealed containers along with silica packets that you can save from manufacturer packaging for shoes, camera film, and many other products.

Preserving seeds
Store seeds away from light, heat, and humidity. Note: Some seeds should be stored in the refrigerator for a while after harvesting and drying. This is

Spanish beans of the 'Scarlet Emperor' variety

I keep my seeds in their original packaging unless I'm harvesting my own. When I'm saving my own seeds, I keep stalks, flower seed heads, and pods in pillowcases, paper bags, or muslin bags while I wait for them to dry. After I extract the seeds, I put them in paper packaging, cloth bags, or jars. If you store your seeds in a jar, be sure to seal it with a perforated lid or open it regularly to let in fresh air.

the case with legume seeds (beans, peas, fava beans), as beetle larvae will feed on them. I highly recommend putting the seeds in the refrigerator for two days and up to one week in order to eliminate larvae that cannot survive the cold temperature.

How Long Vegetable Seeds Remain Viable

A seed's viability means the number of years after harvesting that it is able to germinate. This depends on the species and variety. On the following page, you'll find examples of the average durations that various seeds remain viable.

VEGETABLE	AVERAGE PERIOD OF VIABILITY
Arugula	4 years
Basil	8 years
Bell pepper	3 years
Beet	6 to 10 years
Borage	8 years
Cabbage	5 to 8 years
Cape gooseberry	8 to 10 years
Celery	6 to 8 years
Chervil	2 to 3 years
Chile pepper	3 to 4 years
Cilantro	5 to 6 years
Corn	2 years
Cucumber	8 to 10 years
Dandelion	3 to 4 years
Eggplant	2 to 3 years
Endive	6 to 8 years
Fava bean	5 to 6 years
Fennel	3 to 4 years
Green bean	3 years
Kale	2 to 6 years
Leek	2 to 3 years
Lettuce	4 to 5 years

VEGETABLE	AVERAGE PERIOD OF VIABILITY
Mâche	4 to 5 years
Melon	5 to 6 years
Onion	2 years
Orach	4 to 5 years
Parsley	2 to 3 years
Parsnip	1 to 2 years
Pattypan squash	4 to 5 years
Pea	2 to 3 years
Pumpkin	3 to 4 years
Radish	5 years
Rutabaga	4 to 5 years
Salsify	2 years
Spinach	4 to 5 years
Sunflower	6 to 7 years
Swiss chard	6 years
Tomato	4 to 5 years
Turnip	4 to 5 years
Warrigal greens	3 to 4 years
Watermelon	4 to 5 years
Watercress	3 to 4 years
Zucchini	6 to 8 years

GROWING WITH THE SEASONS

*Harvest of 'Capucine'
(or 'Blauwschokker')
climbing peas*

MY SOWING CALENDAR

In order to optimize my harvests, I begin most plant varieties as seeds, mostly indoors, outdoors if weather permits. For certain varieties, I opt to plant directly in large containers outside as it's much easier.

Given the space constraints on my balcony and two window boxes, I plant in small quantities. This doesn't prevent me from having great diversity, however, so that I can harvest a little of everything.

As I garden all year long, I plant seeds from February to October, reaching a peak at the end of the winter/beginning of spring for spring and summer harvests, then again in the summer to prepare the fall-winter garden. When sowing seeds in summer, make sure to keep the soil moist, but not soggy, until germination. Transplant in the evening and not during the day, especially when the temperature is at its hottest. Water generously, and leave the seedlings in a shady area for a few days after transplanting them to reduce stress.

I'm always eager to start my seedlings in February after a period of relative inactivity during December and January, when I spend time choosing which varieties to plant. In the early days of February, I'm already itching to get started and can't sit still, I'm so excited to start my seeds! I always begin the planting year by sowing bell peppers, chile peppers, and eggplant indoors in seedling trays, as these seeds need warmth to germinate and take a long time to mature. I end the year in October-November, when I plant fava beans, green peas, and garlic directly into containers outside.

These are all general examples. It is important to adapt how you handle seeds in accordance with your region, taking weather conditions into account. Connecting with established gardeners in your area through community gardens or social media can be one of the best ways to learn from years of gardening experience and to make new friends!

THE CLASSIFICATION OF PLANTS

There are two ways to classify the edible plants we grow.

Classification According to the Part of the Plant We Eat

LEAFY GREENS	Lettuce, Swiss chard, endive, mâche, spinach, sorrel, arugula
ROOT AND BULB VEGETABLES	Carrot, beet, fennel, onion, garlic, potato, radish, turnip
FLOWERING VEGETABLES	Cauliflower, broccoli, artichoke
FRUIT AND SEED VEGETABLES	Tomato, green bean, chili pepper, bell pepper, eggplant, fava bean, pea, zucchini

Classification According to Botanical Family

ALLIACEAE	Garlic, shallot, onion, leek
APIACEAE	Carrot, celery, chervil, fennel, parsnip, dill
ASTERACEAE	Artichoke, artichoke thistle, endive, lettuce, dandelion, salsify, sunchoke
BRASSICACEAE	Cabbage, watercress, turnip, radish, arugula, mizuna, horseradish
CHENOPODIACEAE	Beet, spinach, Swiss chard, orach, quinoa
CUCURBITACEAE	Cucumber, zucchini, melon, pumpkin
FABACEAE	Fava bean, green bean, lentil, pea
LAMIACEAE	Basil, mint, marjoram, lemon balm, savory, sage, thyme
SOLANACEAE	Tomato, eggplant, chile pepper, bell pepper, potato, Cape gooseberry

PLANTS FOR CONTAINER GARDENS

Listed here are plants I grow and enjoy in my own container garden. Where possible, I've included notes about different varieties to try.

You'll notice that each plant is named in English with a Latin species name (sometimes called a binomial) after it in parentheses. You can be a wonderful gardener without ever knowing Latin species names, but I've included them here, along with the botanical plant families, so that if you want to be sure what kind of plant you're getting or how it's related to other plants you grow, you can double-check the Latin species name on a seed packet or plant tag.

Each Latin name consists of a first word indicating the genus (like Allium) and a second word known as the specific epithet (like sativum). Together they name the species: *Allium sativum*, or garlic. Where a genus name appears followed by the abbreviation "spp.," it means there are multiple species within that category, for example, chile peppers are *Capiscum* spp. Some Latin names have the genus, the species, then the abbreviation "var." and another adjective (like stalk celery, *Apium graveolens* var. *dulce*) meaning that botanists recognize enough difference between plants of the same species to have created subvarieties.

Some species, like tomato, can include hundreds of cultivars. Cultivars are the names usually listed most prominently on a seed packet and enclosed in single quotation marks: Tomato 'Green Zebra' (*Solanum lycopersicum*).

As discussed on page 17, climates and growing conditions can vary widely across North America, and the varieties and timings that I use in my mild temperate climate may not work for your garden. Refer to climate information at USDA.gov and seek out local resources to find out when gardeners near you have the most success sowing, transplanting, and harvesting.

 = suitable for gardens with less than 6 hours of direct sunlight per day

Arugula growing in my garden

Arugula (*Eruca vesicaria*)

BOTANICAL FAMILY: Brassicaceae
VARIETIES: As with all leafy greens, there are varieties of arugula more or less suited to heat, though even the most heat-resistant (sometimes labeled as "bolt-resistant") arugula won't tolerate many days in a row over 80°F (27°C).

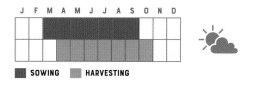

SOWING HARVESTING

Because arugula is very sensitive to heat, I mainly plant at the end of August into early September, preferably straight into a growing container, or if not, in small pots.

The seeds are small, so I simply deposit them on the surface. I scrape the surface lightly with a fork, and gently water. Keep the plants well-watered to prevent extreme bitterness (young leaves are less bitter).

Note that the flowers are edible and taste slightly peppery.

Basil (*Ocimum basilicum*)

BOTANICAL FAMILY: Lamiaceae
VARIETIES: There are many varieties of basil in addition to what you might picture as classic green Italian sweet basil. Basil, like its relative, mint, comes in many varieties with special aromas, such as lemon, cinnamon, and even Christmas basil, which is reminiscent of pine!

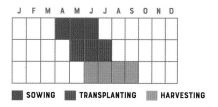

SOWING TRANSPLANTING HARVESTING

I sow basil in warm weather as early as the first days of April, or sometimes, like in 2020, a year with an exceptionally mild spring, in the second half of March.

Once the first true leaves have emerged on the seedlings, I start with an intermediary transplant to larger growing containers, then transplant them to the foot of the tomato stem after the middle of May.

During the summer, I propagate more basil plants by stripping two or three 3-inch (7.5 cm) stems until there are only two or three leaves at the top. Then I place them in water near a window. Roots appear in a few days. Once they're well-developed, I transplant the cuttings.

Beans (*Phaseolus vulgaris*)

BOTANICAL FAMILY: Fabaceae

VARIETIES: There are many container-friendly cultivars within both the pole bean (meaning climbing or vining) and bush bean varieties.

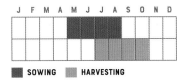

J	F	M	A	M	J	J	A	S	O	N	D
				■	■	■	■				
						▨	▨	▨			

■ SOWING   ▨ HARVESTING

'Blauhilde' pole beans

Growing beans is easy and fast. In a small garden, the advantage of pole beans—whether grown to eat fresh or dried—is that they can be grown on stakes and don't need a lot of space. Green beans are sensitive to the cold and frosts, so I plant mine from mid-May onward, directly into their final growing container, five seeds at a time at a reduced distance of about 8 inches (20 cm) apart. I soak the seeds beforehand for 12 hours. Then I cover them with soil, pat it down, and water.

About two weeks after they appear, I start to build up soil around their stems. Corn and cucurbitaceous plants (like cucumbers and squash) are traditionally partnered with pole beans. This beneficial association (sometimes called "guilds" in permaculture) was developed by Indigenous farmers in the Americas and is still used. In Latin America, this combination is called Milpa, and in North America, it is more often referred to as the Three Sisters. Plant some corn and when it reaches 12 to 16 inches (30 to 40 cm) tall, plant the pole beans around the stem of the corn. At the same time that you plant the beans, add a zucchini or squash plant in the remaining space. The zucchini preserves the humidity at the base of the corn stalk, which acts as a stake for the climbing beans, which, in turn, like all legumes, enrich the soil with nitrogen. This association can be helpful in a small garden as it optimizes space.

Harvesting 'Rocbrun' and 'Cupidon' dwarf beans

Beet (*Beta vulgaris*)

BOTANICAL FAMILY: Chenopodiaceae

VARIETIES: Beets come in colors from pale gold to deepest purple, and there are also miniature varieties well-suited to smaller containers.

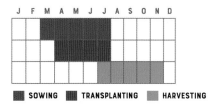

J F M A M J J A S O N D

■ SOWING ■ TRANSPLANTING ■ HARVESTING

Beets are easy to grow. Each seed is actually a cluster, containing three or four seeds, so each cluster results in several seedlings. I sow as early as March in small pots outside or protected under horticultural fleece on the balcony or windowsill. I transplant each plant 4.5 to 5 inches (11.5 to 13 cm) apart once they have germinated two true leaves. The beet is one of the few root vegetables that is easy to transplant.

Borage (*Borage officinalis*)

BOTANICAL FAMILY: Boraginaceae

VARIETIES: Borage is available with blue or white flowers.

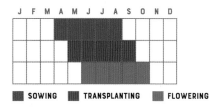

J F M A M J J A S O N D

■ SOWING ■ TRANSPLANTING ■ FLOWERING

Borage is a nectar-rich plant that is very easy to grow. Sow it once and you'll always have borage growing in your garden, as it reseeds freely. It has a very short growth cycle, and you can easily see three harvests in one year. It's a plant I don't sow much anymore as I am happy to just let the existing plants self-sow into the patch of soil where I want them to grow, or I put them in small pots to give as gifts. I plant borage seeds from April to June, outside in small pots or straight into larger growing containers.

Cabbages and Asian Mustards (*Brassica* spp.)

BOTANICAL FAMILY: Brassicaceae

VARIETIES: There are a rainbow of cabbage and Asian greens available for the adventurous grower. Do keep in mind that a single head of cabbage takes up an enormous amount of space, so you may want to focus more on loose leaf cabbages like Napa, bok choy, kale, or Asian mustards that can even be grown on a windowsill and harvested as microgreens.

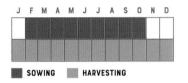

I opt for cabbage varieties chosen for their leaves, such as kale and Chinese cabbage, which take up relatively little room in the vegetable garden, as well as Asian mustards. I do indulge my taste for round cabbage and Romanesco, though given the size of my vegetable garden, I grow only one plant in fall and winter.

I plant cabbage seeds in a small pot or tray at the time prescribed for each variety. I follow with an intermediary transplant into individual containers once two true leaves have sprouted before putting them in their permanent place in the garden once they are a bit fleshed out.

Calendula (*Calendula officinalis*)

BOTANICAL FAMILY: Asteraceae

VARIETIES: Bright orange is the classic calendula color, but some cultivars in pale yellow and even dusty pink have been introduced in recent years if you're not a fan of orange!

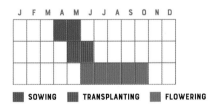

I plant calendula seeds directly into the garden at the first signs of spring. Like poppies, they don't mind cold soil and benefit from the early start. I cover the seeds with soil and keep them moist until they germinate. Calendula is particularly useful in vegetable gardens because it attracts numerous pollinating insects and keeps aphids at bay. I remove the wilted flowers to assure continuous blooming. In August, I let the plants go to seed so that they will reseed for next year.

While they don't have a strong flavor, calendula petals are highly valued for being vitamin-rich. They also make a colorful addition to salads, or even as sprinkles on a cake!

Carrot (*Daucus carota* subsp. *sativus*)

BOTANICAL FAMILY: Apiaceae

VARIETIES: Carrots come in a variety of colors, lengths, and even shapes. Unless you have a very deep container to plant in, though, you'll have the most success with round and short varieties.

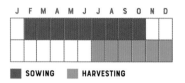

■ SOWING ■ HARVESTING

I sow these seeds directly into the containers where they'll grow until harvest, since carrots do not take well to transplanting. I plant in parallel grooves spaced about 8 to 10 inches (20 to 25 cm) apart. Carrot seeds are tiny, and I make sure not to plant too many, ideally just over 1 inch (2.5 cm) apart. I cover them with a thin layer of soil, pat down, and then water delicately. Carrots take a long time to germinate, around three weeks, and their soil must remain moist. In order to conserve moisture, I cover my seeds with a thick piece of cardboard. I check for germination every day and as soon as the seeds germinate, I remove the cardboard. I thin out the seedlings by snipping the extras at the base of the stem using garden shears, so that I have one placed every 2 to 3 inches (5 to 7.5 cm).

In my climate, I'm able to plant fast-growing varieties such as 'Paris market' as early as February under frost-protective horticultural fleece, in sifted earth with no clumps so that the seedlings don't hit any obstacles during their development.

Harvest of multicolored chards

Celery (*Apium graveolens*)

BOTANICAL FAMILY: Apiaceae

VARIETIES: The three main varieties of celery are stalk or Pascal celery (*Apium graveolens* var. *dulce*), the kind most commonly sold in American grocery stores and usually eaten raw; leaf celery (*Apium graveolens* var. *secalinum*), which has smaller stalks and more robustly flavored leaves; and the variety known most commonly as celeriac (*Apium graveolens* var. *rapaceum*), which is grown for its starchy root and stem and requires a long growing season.

I sprinkle celery seeds in a small pot, covering them with about an eighth of an inch (3 mm) of finely sifted soil because the seeds are very small. I pat the soil down and delicately water (with a mister or capillary action as described on page 79). I transplant the seedlings farther apart once there are three to four leaves, then move them to the balcony once there are six to eight leaves, giving each plant 12 inches (30 cm) of space to grow in every direction.

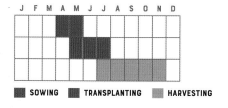

J F M A M J J A S O N D

■ SOWING ■ TRANSPLANTING ■ HARVESTING

Chard (*Beta vulgaris* var. *cicla*)

BOTANICAL FAMILY: Chenopodiaceae

VARIETIES: While not distinct in taste from varieties with plain white stems, rainbow chard with red, yellow, and pink stalks is a beautiful addition to your garden and plate!

I sow chard as early as March, in small pots on my balcony, protected under horticultural fleece. I transplant each plant 4.5 to 5 inches (11.5 to 13 cm) apart once they have germinated two true leaves. The leaves can be eaten in salad when young or as cooked greens when mature.

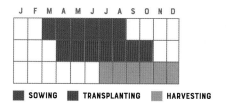

J F M A M J J A S O N D

■ SOWING ■ TRANSPLANTING ■ HARVESTING

Chervil (*Anthriscus cerefolium*)

BOTANICAL FAMILY: Apiaceae

VARIETIES: Chervil, like its relative, parsley, comes in varieties with either curly or flat leaves.

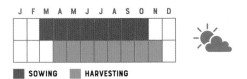

■ SOWING   ■ HARVESTING

I stagger my sowings of chervil from April to October, about every three to four weeks, because it goes to seed very quickly. To avoid having the plant produce seeds too early, keep its soil moist and away from extreme heat. I sprinkle seeds in small quantities straight into their container in the garden or in small pots, making sure to space the plants out. I cover the seeds with a thin layer of soil, pat down, and then water. I keep the soil moist until the chervil germinates. You can also plant the seeds in small pots; once the seedlings have four true leaves, I transplant the plant and the root ball, preferably into a shady spot. I harvest after five to six weeks of growth.

Chicory/Endive (*Cichorium* spp.)

BOTANICAL FAMILY: Asteraceae

VARIETIES: This group of plants includes Belgian endive, French endive, and radicchio.

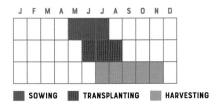

■ SOWING   ■ TRANSPLANTING   ■ HARVESTING

Chicory and endive seeds are tiny. I sow them in rows, in a tray, in finely sifted potting soil barely covering the seeds. I pat them down to make sure they're in contact with the soil, then I water them through capillary action by soaking the trays from the bottom. I sow outdoors, from March onward. I transplant into individual containers once the seedlings have two true leaves and then transplant them again into larger pots once they have developed sufficiently.

Chives (*Allium schoenoprasum*)

BOTANICAL FAMILY: Alliaceae

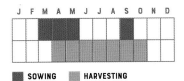

■ SOWING ■ HARVESTING

I sprinkle a few seeds to grow a lovely bouquet, spacing them out around 0.5 inches (1.25 cm) in a small container outside. I transplant the clump once the plants have developed sufficiently—around two months later—and if I have several, at a distance of about 12 inches (30 cm) apart.

After a few growing seasons, I increase my yield by dividing the clump. To do this, I unearth it, keeping as many roots intact as possible, and then I divide it into several clumps that I transplant. I water copiously to facilitate the new plants' growth. I let the plants settle in for about fifteen days before I start harvesting again, which I do often to stimulate the growth of more leaves. Chives are perennials so they last several years in the garden, even in very cold climates.

Cilantro (*Coriandrum sativum*)

BOTANICAL FAMILY: Apiaceae
VARIETIES: There are varieties of cilantro (such as Vietnamese or Moroccan) that have been developed for different growing conditions around the world, especially warmer climates.

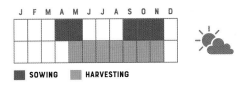

■ SOWING ■ HARVESTING

I sow cilantro seeds often as they go to seed very quickly. I plant the seeds in a small pot and keep them warm inside, and then move them outside under a cover in April, and into the final spot in the garden from May onward. I transplant out of the small pots after the plant germinates two or three true leaves. I harvest regularly to encourage the plants to grow leaves. Planted next to carrots, cilantro characteristically keeps the carrot rust flies away.

Corn (*Zea mays*)

BOTANICAL FAMILY: Poaceae

VARIETIES: You can grow both corn to eat fresh from the cob and corn that's good for drying to make into popcorn!

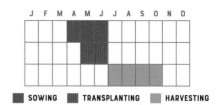

J	F	M	A	M	J	J	A	S	O	N	D
				▓	▓						
					▓						
							▓	▓	▓	▓	

■ SOWING   ▓ TRANSPLANTING   ▒ HARVESTING

'Glass Gem' corn

I either plant corn in small pots, spacing the seeds out, or I plant them in a row in a tray. I transplant them into their place in the garden when the stalks are about 6 to 8 inches (15 to 20 cm) tall.

Keep in mind that corn is wind-pollinated, so it should be planted in circles or blocks (rather than rows), especially when you have only a few plants, to assure optimal pollination and cob formation.

Cosmos (*Cosmos bipinnatus*)

BOTANICAL FAMILY: Asteraceae

VARIETIES: Cosmos comes in a variety of heights and colors, from pure white to deep purple, with plenty of pinks and even some yellows in between. You can buy seed mixes with multiple colors or choose single colors to suit a certain design scheme.

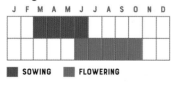

J	F	M	A	M	J	J	A	S	O	N	D
			▓	▓	▓						
					▒	▒	▒	▒			

■ SOWING   ▒ FLOWERING

I love cosmos, an annual flower that's very easy to grow and produces luminous, colorful blooms that attract pollinators.

I sow repeatedly through the spring and summer until July, and scatter the seeds randomly in small containers, spacing them out about 0.5 inches (1.25 cm) apart in order to grow a tuft. I transplant the clumps, each made up of a few plants, to get a better visual effect. I remove the wilted flowers often (this is called "deadheading") to encourage the plant to grow more.

Cucamelon (*Melothria scabra*), also known as Mouse Melon or Mexican Sour Cucumber

BOTANICAL FAMILY: Cucurbitaceae

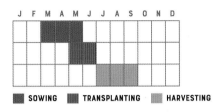

J F M A M J J A S O N D

■ SOWING　　■ TRANSPLANTING　　■ HARVESTING

Cucamelon

Cucamelon is a great alternative to cucumber because of the small amount of space that the plant takes up. This is a perennial that originated in the tropics but you can also grow it as an annual. It yields charming, small oblong fruit, just a bit bigger than cherries, with skins that are striped dark green and white.

I plant three seeds to a pot, in a warm environment, after the second half of April. Once the seedlings have developed, after germinating three to four true leaves, I move them to their permanent spot. I train the plant to grow on vertical stakes. As it grows, the plant produces tendrils. If need be, I help it start climbing by guiding it on stakes and loosely attaching the stalks with string in such a way as not to damage them.

Cucumber (*Cucumis sativus*)

BOTANICAL FAMILY: Cucurbitaceae

VARIETIES: Miniature Persian or pickling cucumber varieties are perfect for container growing.

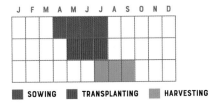

J F M A M J J A S O N D

■ SOWING ■ TRANSPLANTING ■ HARVESTING

I plant cucumbers in the second half of April or in early May. I add just a single seed to each small pot, which I fill with a mixture of potting soil and compost in order to feed the nutrient-hungry fruiting plant. I keep the cucumber indoors, close to heat and lots of light, until two or three true leaves appear when I transplant it to the balcony. I train the cucumber plant to climb a three-legged teepee to save space. I attach the legs of the teepee together with a string spiral, starting at the bottom and working up. As the cucumber plant grows, its thin, spiraling tendrils attach themselves to the string.

Eggplant (*Solanum melongena*)

BOTANICAL FAMILY: Solanaceae

VARIETIES: Small eggplant varieties that grow in clusters are particularly well-suited to growing in containers.

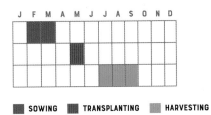

J F M A M J J A S O N D

■ SOWING ■ TRANSPLANTING ■ HARVESTING

Eggplant is one of the first plants I start in early February because it grows slowly. I sow three to four seeds in small pots that I place near a radiator, as eggplant needs to be kept at a temperature above 68°F (20°C) in order to germinate.

As soon as the first real leaves emerge, I transplant each seedling into individual pots. Fifteen days before I move them to the balcony, I gradually toughen the plants up by moving them outside for longer and longer periods of time. I typically start by leaving them outside for one hour the first day, two hours the second day, and so on. After mid-May, I transplant them into their final position.

Fava Beans (*Vicia faba*), also known as Broad Beans

BOTANICAL FAMILY: Fabaceae

VARIETIES: You can select small or large pod varieties of fava beans. The smaller kind bears more pods per cluster than the large variety.

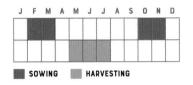

Fava beans are a legume, the delicious flavor of which I discovered when I started growing them. After experimenting a few times ever since 2014 to determine the best time to plant in my climate, I sow fava beans in October or, at the latest, the first few days of November for a May harvest. Fava beans then cede their place to tomatoes in near-perfect timing. Depending on your Hardiness Zone and weather conditions, you can also plant fava beans in spring from the second half of February until April.

I plant the seeds in rows about 12 to 16 inches (30 to 40 cm) apart, with one seed every 2 inches (5 cm), in holes about 2 inches (5 cm) deep. I pat down and water.

Once the plant reaches about 6 inches (15 cm) tall, I build the soil up around the stem. This protects and keeps the roots firmly in the ground. Another thing you can do is place stakes in the four corners of the planter and tie them together with string as the plant grows. Fava beans are susceptible to aphids, but planting dill alongside seems to help keep them at bay.

Fennel (*Foeniculum vulgare*)

BOTANICAL FAMILY: Apiaceae

VARIETIES: Fennel is usually divided into the categories of common and sweet, best used as herbs or as a spice from the dried seeds, and bulb or Florence fennel, with stems that thicken at the base, which can be cooked as a vegetable.

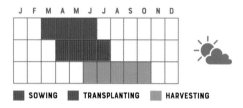

J F M A M J J A S O N D

■ SOWING ■ TRANSPLANTING ■ HARVESTING

I plant fennel in pots or planters, scattered or in rows. Around six weeks after sowing, when four to five true leaves have germinated, I transplant them to a container, about 6 inches (15 cm) apart. If you don't have enough space or sunlight for fennel bulbs to form, the greens are a delicious aromatic herb that can be cut throughout the growing year.

Fennel is perennial in many climates and pollinators love the flowers. Additionally, bronze fennel is one of the best host plants for black swallowtail butterfly caterpillars. Swallowtail pupa will sometimes overwinter on fennel plants and songbirds forage the seedheads, so if you live in a place with cold winters, it's a good idea to leave dead fennel stems and seed heads in place throughout the winter for wildlife until the new growth starts to emerge in the spring. (You won't get bulbs or many flowers, but you can get plenty of soft foliage to use as an herb.)

Four O'Clocks (*Mirabilis jalapa*)

BOTANICAL FAMILY: Nyctaginaceae

VARIETIES: Four O'Clocks come in lots of bright colors, and you can also seek out variegated ones whose petals are streaked with multiple colors.

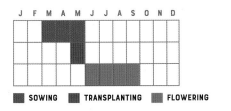

■ SOWING ■ TRANSPLANTING ■ FLOWERING

I plant Four O'Clock seeds in a small pot after soaking them for 12 hours, sometime during the second half of March. I then proceed with an intermediary transplant before I add them to my container garden. This fast-growing plant produces a multitude of flowers that bloom toward the end of the day, between 4:00 and 6:00 PM, hence their name, "four o'clock." They droop by morning. As a result, they offer an abundant food source for evening pollinators like moths, though any hummingbirds out later in the day will also be delighted to find them! I regularly remove the faded flowers so that the plant continues to produce more. At the end of the season, I let the plant make seeds that will be used for the next year.

NOTE: Four O'Clocks are toxic to people and pets. I plant them because they encourage nocturnal pollinators, but use caution if you have small children or pets that like to nibble on plants.

Garlic (*Allium sativum*)

BOTANICAL FAMILY: Alliaceae

VARIETIES: Softneck (including artichoke and silverskin, and other varieties) and hardneck (including porcelain, rocambole, purple stripe, and other varieties).

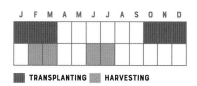

J	F	M	A	M	J	J	A	S	O	N	D

■ TRANSPLANTING   ■ HARVESTING

Garlic presents itself as a head made up of several cloves. Garlic produces either green shoots you can harvest from still-growing plants—when the bulb is about three months old and hasn't yet formed—to put in omelets and salads, or a full head by the end of the growing season. Growers typically divide all garlics into two main categories: hardneck, which has a strong central flower stalk, thicker skin, and is better for colder climates, and softneck, which has thinner skin and is more suited to milder winter temperatures.

To grow my garlic, I buy heads of locally grown white garlic at an organic shop. I favor the largest, firmest, and healthiest heads with nice-looking cloves. I plant only the largest cloves from the outside of the head, which are more productive than the smaller ones in the center. I grow it in regular-size window boxes, as root development is less important. I trace a straight line in the soil and plant the cloves by pushing them into the earth every 4 inches (10 cm), about 1 to 1.5 inches (3 to 4 cm) below the surface. I make sure to plant the cloves with their pointed tips upright.

Research garlic planting times for your region, factoring in that cold temperatures will be more extreme in containers. Just remember that some winter cold is essential to hardneck garlic's development.

Autumnal rains and the constant humidity in Paris allow me to forgo watering my garlic over winter. Nonetheless, I make sure the plant doesn't sit in water because an excess can rot the cloves.

I harvest garlic shoots in early spring and the garlic heads at the beginning of the summer when the foliage/leaves are dried out. I let the heads dry out for a few more days when the weather is dry before storing them in a cool and well-ventilated room.

Garlic Chives (*Allium tuberosum*)

BOTANICAL FAMILY: Alliaceae

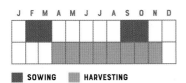

	J	F	M	A	M	J	J	A	S	O	N	D

- SOWING
- HARVESTING

The garlic chive is a perennial herb with a slight taste of garlic, and its leaves are thicker than regular chives and produce pretty white flowers. You grow and transplant them the same way you do chives (see page 111), although, unlike regular chives, garlic chives form bulbs that are also edible. Personally, I harvest only the leaves by cutting the plant down to the base. This way the leaves will regrow for a more perpetual yield than I'd get if I dug up the bulbs.

Hyssop (*Hyssopus officinalis*)

BOTANICAL FAMILY: Lamiaceae

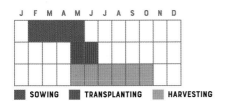

	J	F	M	A	M	J	J	A	S	O	N	D

- SOWING
- TRANSPLANTING
- HARVESTING

The hyssop is a pretty nectar-rich plant with vivid blue flowers.

In March and April, I sprinkle the seeds randomly in small pots indoors, under about 0.5 inch (1.25 cm) of soil, and outdoors from May onward. I do an intermediary transplant into individual pots once the seedlings are 1.5 to 2 inches (4 to 5 cm) tall. I plant them in the garden when they reach 6 to 8 inches (15 to 20 cm) high.

It's possible to divide the clumps to multiply your hyssop plants in the same way you would chives (see page 111) from March to September.

Hyssop is perennial and can tolerate cold temperatures, especially if the roots are kept moist but not soaking during freezing temperatures.

Korean Mint (*Agastache rugosa*)

BOTANICAL FAMILY: Lamiaceae

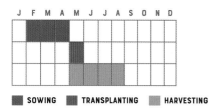

| | SOWING | | TRANSPLANTING | | HARVESTING |

I have a particular fondness for this ornamental and aromatic plant whose leaves have a delicious scent and anise flavor—and pollinators love the flowers.

I sow Korean Mint in a warm place in a small tray or pot. I barely cover the seeds as they need light to germinate. I first transplant them into individual pots once the seedlings germinate true leaves. Then I transplant once again in mid-May, after there is no danger of frost, to their permanent place in the garden.

Lacy Phacelia (*Phacelia tanacetifolia*)

BOTANICAL FAMILY: Hydrophyllaceae

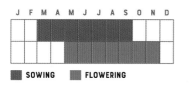

| | SOWING | | FLOWERING |

Phacelia is a fast-growing cover crop (see page 84) with magnificent bluish-mauve flowers that are favored by pollinators, which is the main reason I grow it. Phacelia seeds are very small, and I plant them straight into the garden, randomly, on the surface of a growing tray. I lightly scrape the surface of the soil with a fork so that the seeds are just a few millimeters into the soil. I pat down and water very gently, keeping the surface moist until germination. The plant will flower around eight weeks after planting. In order to have recurring blooms, I stagger sowing all season long.

Leek (*Allium porrum*)

BOTANICAL FAMILY: Allicaceae

VARIETIES: As with their relatives onions and garlic, there are tender (summer) and more cold-hardy (winter) varieties of leeks. Depending on your Hardiness Zone, you may be able to grow both varieties, or have to confine yourself to just one.

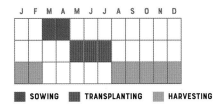

	J	F	M	A	M	J	J	A	S	O	N	D
			■									
					■	■						
	■							■	■	■	■	■

■ SOWING   ■ TRANSPLANTING   ■ HARVESTING

I usually plant winter leek seeds in a small pot or tray, randomly or in rows, at the beginning of spring. I transplant them into their permanent placement once they're the size and thickness of a pencil.

Lettuce (*Lactuca sativa*)

BOTANICAL FAMILY: Asteraceae

VARIETIES: Lettuce comes in hundreds of varieties, including those suited to cold or hot weather, in colors from deep purple to pale yellow, and in varieties best to harvest as individual leaves or to let mature and pick as a head.

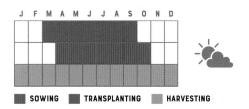

SOWING   TRANSPLANTING   HARVESTING

Except in the coldest winters, you can grow lettuce all year, as long as you choose varieties that lend themselves to it and you have some horticultural fleece on hand to protect young plants if snow starts to fall. I begin the process with spring lettuce seeds from the end of February to early March, summer lettuces in May, and I sow fall and winter lettuces in August. I also plant all-season cut-and-come-again lettuces. To extend your lettuce growing season into hotter summers, provide plenty of water and shade for the plants during the hottest hours of the afternoon to help keep the leaves from becoming bitter.

I plant in small pots or trays, scattered or in rows, making sure to space the seeds out so that the seedlings have enough room to grow. I cover them with a very fine layer of soil, keeping it damp until germination. Once two true leaves have appeared, I transplant them into individual containers or in their permanent spot in the garden, making sure not to cover the neck or the base of the leaves.

You can also scatter seed directly in the final growing container.

Lettuce doesn't need a lot of space for its roots as long as it receives plenty of water. You can cut a few leaves from each plant and then let them regrow, assuring a perpetual harvest from one sowing across several months.

Mâche (*Valerianella locusta*), also known as Corn Salad

BOTANICAL FAMILY: Valerianaceae

VARIETIES: As with most leafy vegetables, you can seek out either cold-hardy or heat-hardy varieties of mâche, depending on your climate and when you hope to harvest.

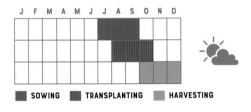

I usually plant mâche in a tray because there's not enough room in the garden between August and September. I place three to four seeds in each of the tray's cells. I cover the seeds with a thin layer of sifted soil, pat down, and water delicately.

I transplant each clump to its permanent place in the garden without thinning out so that I end up with nice bouquets of mâche around only 4 inches (10 cm) apart.

Marigold (*Tagetes* spp.)

BOTANICAL FAMILY: Asteraceae

VARIETIES: Marigold varieties range from huge pom-poms to tiny florets, from deep rusty red to pale cream. When selecting marigold seeds, choosing a variety that has pistils and stamens surrounded by petals rather than the kinds that are all petals will supply food for pollinators.

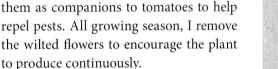

I plant marigolds in a small pot or tray, scattered or in rows. Once two true leaves have appeared, I transplant them into individual pots. When I transplant them into the vegetable garden, I mainly plant them as companions to tomatoes to help repel pests. All growing season, I remove the wilted flowers to encourage the plant to produce continuously.

My harvest on April 18, 2020, during the COVID-19 lockdown: 'Red Ursa' kale, blood sorrel, 'Mouchetée de Salasc' lettuce, and 'Rouge de Vérone' chicory

My harvest on March 31, 2020, during lockdown: calendula and arugula flowers, parsley, 'Blood Sorrel,' garlic chives, 'Grenoble Red' lettuce leaves, and black radish microgreens

Onion (*Allium cepa*)

BOTANICAL FAMILY: Alliaceae

VARIETIES: There are onion varieties planted in summer for harvesting the following spring, or in spring for autumn harvest. Many onion varieties can withstand cold winters if they don't sit in soggy soil; just be sure to check the Hardiness Zone range on the seed packet.

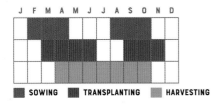

I plant small white onion seeds (sometimes known as "pickling onions") in small pots or a tray, either randomly sprinkled or in a row, from mid-August to mid-September. I transplant them into the garden between mid-October and mid-November. I can harvest them as early as the following spring. Planting autumn-harvested onion seeds is the same process. In this case however, I plant in March and transplant in May–June for a September–October harvest.

Orach (*Atriplex hortensis*)

BOTANICAL FAMILY: Chenopodiaceae

VARIETIES: While green orach is the most obvious choice if you grow orach as a warm-weather crop, you can also choose purple or pale blond orach—or an assortment of colors.

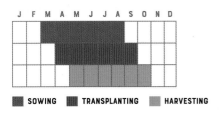

I cultivate purple orach, whose leaves are decorative as well as edible, as early as March in small pots outside. I barely cover the seeds as they need light to germinate. I transplant into individual growing containers when the first two true leaves appear. Once it reaches 1 foot (30 cm) tall, I pinch the plant—by which I mean I remove the tip of the main stalk with my thumb and index finger—so that it gets bushy and develops more branches. Growing orach is very easy and this vegetable is heat tolerant and can easily replace spinach during the summer. It may be a great option for you if summer heat hits early where you live.

Parsley (*Petroselinum crispum*)

BOTANICAL FAMILY: Apiaceae

VARIETIES: As with chervil (see page 110), most parsley cultivars are classified either as flat-leaf, which holds its flavor better when cooked, or curly-leaf, which has more fibrous leaves that hold their shape even when chopped finely.

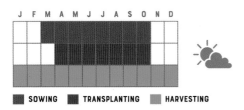

J F M A M J J A S O N D

█ SOWING █ TRANSPLANTING █ HARVESTING

Planting parsley is easy, but germination can take a while. To accelerate the process, you can soak the seeds for 12 to 24 hours and then spread them out on a paper towel to make the seeds easier to handle (just don't leave the soaked seeds to dry out completely!).

I sow parsley outdoors from March onward, randomly sprinkled in small pots or in rows in a tray, in finely sifted potting soil. I barely cover the seeds. I just pat them down to make sure they're in contact with the soil and water by soaking the trays from the bottom (see page 50) if possible. I water regularly to keep the soil damp until germination, which can take from fifteen days to three weeks after planting. Once three to four leaves have appeared, I transplant the clump without thinning it out for a pretty bouquet in my garden.

Parsley likes cool, even cold weather, though if temperatures reach below freezing, it will need some protection—either cover it with horticultural fleece or put it inside by a cold window.

Peas (*Pisum sativum*)

BOTANICAL FAMILY: Fabaceae

VARIETIES: There are pea varieties that can be eaten with the pod before the seeds mature (sometimes called "snow peas" or "mangetout"), pea pods that are delicious eaten whole with plump peas inside (sometimes called "sugar snaps") and others, shelling peas, that have tough pods. There are even peas with purple pods, which have the advantage of being easier to see and pick.

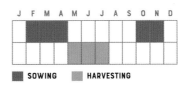

J	F	M	A	M	J	J	A	S	O	N	D
		■	■						■	■	
				■	■						

■ SOWING ■ HARVESTING

Planting peas is very simple. To maximize production in my mild climate, I plant climbing pea varieties in October, early November at the latest, for a May harvest, just before tomato planting begins. I soak the seeds for 12 hours before sowing. In the meantime, I prepare the teepees, if they're not already in place, to support the plant as it grows.

I sow a five-seed pocket at the foot of each stake.

If your winters are colder than mine, keep in mind that peas do best in cool weather, and, like poppies, can be sown directly outside even when there's still a chance of frost in spring.

Pea seeds can be very attractive to rodents and birds. If you have trouble with animals digging up your peas, a layer of sturdy wire mesh over the soil can help.

Peppers (Chile and Bell; *Capiscum* spp.)

BOTANICAL FAMILY: Solanaceae

VARIETIES: While the taste difference between a bell pepper and a chile pepper like cayenne is wildly different, they are closely related and require similar growing conditions. When choosing pepper varieties, you can estimate the amount of heat each one produces by looking up the variety's Scoville units. To give you an idea of the range, a bell pepper is zero units, jalapeños range between two thousand and eight thousand units, while a ghost pepper is upward of one million Scoville units!

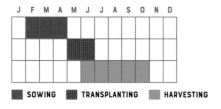

I sow peppers from February until March, in small pots or trays in the warm indoors. I place the containers near a radiator to help germination, as chile peppers and bell peppers, like their relative, eggplant, need warmth to germinate and take a long time to mature.

Once the plant has its first two true leaves, I transplant the seedlings into individual pots. Fifteen days before transplanting outside, I slowly increase their hardiness by getting them used to their new environment. I do this by setting the plants outside in a shaded spot on warm days, taking them in at night and gradually increasing the amount of sunlight the plants receive each day.

Poppy (*Papaver* spp.)

BOTANICAL FAMILY: Papaveraceae

VARIETIES: There are many kinds of poppies from all around the world, including Breadseed, Icelandic, Shirley, and California. They are all beloved by pollinators, and there's one suited for almost every climate, from bitterly cold to tropical temperatures.

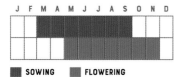

I sow poppy seeds indoors, spacing the seeds out in small pots, between March and April. Covering the seeds lightly with soil, I pat them down and water, preferably by soaking the pots from the bottom (see page 50). I keep the soil moist until germination, then transplant the clump whole, without thinning it out, as poppies have very sensitive roots.

Breadseed and Icelandic poppies also take well to being sown directly outside while there's still frost in the forecast. Scatter them here and there in March or early April in cold climates, and even if there are several snows to come, they'll germinate strongly when they're ready.

Potato (*Solanum tuberosum*)

BOTANICAL FAMILY: Solanaceae

VARIETIES: Like their relatives, tomatoes, potatoes come in a range of sizes and a rainbow of colors from palest white through yellow and red to dark purple. There are also widely varying potato textures, from waxy to starchy. When growing potatoes in small spaces, it can be beneficial to pick a kind that can be harvested earlier in the summer (usually referred to as "early potatoes") to free up space for other crops.

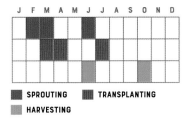

J	F	M	A	M	J	J	A	S	O	N	D
	■		■								
		■	■		■						
				▨			▨				

■ SPROUTING   ■ TRANSPLANTING
▨ HARVESTING

'Bleue de la Manche' potato

I buy my first potato tubers as early as January–February from an organic store, so they won't have been sprayed with anti-germinating hormones. I place them in a bright cool room so that their eyes develop stocky sprouts.

I watch the weather and plant outside as early as March if it's a mild spring, as it was in 2020. Otherwise, I wait until April.

I save empty potting soil bags to use as growing containers, poking holes with a fork so water can drain well, then I half-fill the bag with soil and compost or composted manure, rolling the sides of the bag down to just a few inches above the soil surface.

I plant three tubers per bag approximately 4 to 6 inches (10 to 15 cm) deep, their sprouts pointing up. I cover with a layer of soil, prop the bag upright in a sunny place outside, and water.

Once the stalks reach 8 to 10 inches (20 to 25 cm), I form a mound of soil around them by rolling up the sides of the bag and adding more soil. I repeat this several times, rolling up the edges of the bag as it fills, until harvest—around three months after planting.

You can harvest a few at a time by reaching your hand into the bag and feeling around for tubers, or harvest them all at once, by tipping the contents of the bag out.

Radish (*Raphanus sativus*)

BOTANICAL FAMILY: Brassicaceae

VARIETIES: Spring radishes are a famously speedy crop: You can harvest them just over a month after planting. Winter radishes are cold-hardy in milder climates like mine but take longer to mature. They tend to be denser and not as sweet and, after harvesting, can be stored for longer than spring radishes. Many Asian radish varieties are classed as winter radishes. Neither kind of radish does well when the temperature is consistently above 80°F (27°C) every day.

As I'm fonder of winter turnips than radishes, I plant just a few seeds of winter radish out of curiosity and to discover new varieties. I plant them directly into their permanent container in August, leaving about 3 inches (7.5 cm) between the seeds.

I sow spring radishes every month, staggered, as early as March, directly into the growing container, 1.5 inches (4 cm) apart. I water regularly to obtain milder-tasting radishes. I harvest five to six weeks after planting.

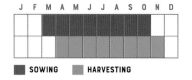

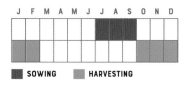

Scabiosa or Pincushion Flower (*Scabiosa* spp.)

BOTANICAL FAMILY: Caprifoliaceae

VARIETIES: There are many different species of scabiosa from different parts of the world that vary in height and color, but no matter their size, most come in either white or shades of purple.

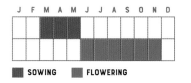

While not poisonous, scabiosa don't have much flavor and are a treat for pollinators rather than humans. I plant scabiosa at the first signs of spring, usually scattering them in a tray for the lack of space in my container garden. I cover them very lightly with soil, pat down, and water. I keep the soil moist until the seeds germinate. I transplant the seedlings into individual pots once they are developed enough for me to place them in their permanent container in the garden in May. To encourage continuing blooms, I regularly remove the wilted flowers.

Shallot (*Allium cepa* var. *aggregatum*)

BOTANICAL FAMILY: Alliaceous

VARIETIES: French gray shallots are considered the most aromatic variety, but you can also get varieties classed as round, semi-long, and long. French gray shallots are planted from October to February and round, semi-long, and long from February to April.

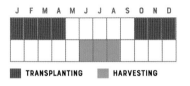

J F M A M J J A S O N D

TRANSPLANTING   HARVESTING

I plant shallots year-round for their edible green leaves. You can get shallot bulbs in early fall from organic farmers (just as with garlic) and plant them directly in their final positions.

Plant in rows 12 inches (30 cm) apart, placing bulbs about 4 inches (10 cm) apart from each other with their pointed tips upright and the roots down (as with garlic). One trick for gaining space in a window box is to plant in staggered rows. I pat the soil so that the bulbs are in close contact with the earth and water after planting unless rain is in the forecast. I harvest the bulbs in the summertime once the leaves begin to dry.

Sorrel (*Rumex acetosa* and *R. scutatus*)

BOTANICAL FAMILY: Polygonaceae

VARIETIES: While not available in as many colors as lettuce, there are varieties of sorrel with red or purple veins that can add welcome color to your spring salad bowl.

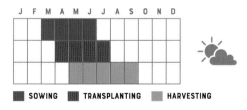

J F M A M J J A S O N D

SOWING   TRANSPLANTING   HARVESTING

Sorrel is more widely eaten in Europe than America but is gaining popularity. It has a zingy, almost citrusy taste, and is delicious raw when the leaves are young and tender, or as a cooked green when mature.

I sow sorrel randomly scattered in small pots or in a tray in rows. I cover lightly with potting soil and keep the mound damp until the seeds germinate. I make an intermediary transplant into individual pots after two true leaves have germinated then into the vegetable garden once there are around four to five leaves.

Spinach (*Spinacia oleracea*)

BOTANICAL FAMILY: Chenopodiaceae

VARIETIES: As with many leafy greens, some spinach cultivars are bred to handle heat, while others are more cold-resilient.

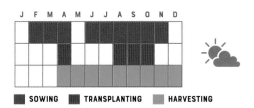

	J	F	M	A	M	J	J	A	S	O	N	D

■ SOWING   ■ TRANSPLANTING   ■ HARVESTING

I sow my spinach indoors as early as February, and then outside starting in March and April. Summer spinach (varieties well-suited to long days and warmer temperatures) is sown from June to September and fall-winter spinach from mid-August to November.

Spinach is susceptible to stress from transplanting, so I favor planting in a seedling tray, in soil blocks I buy from a garden center, or directly into its final growing position. Growing like this makes it possible to transplant without disturbing the roots too much. I sow two or three seeds for each cell, or in grooves just about 0.5 inches (1.25 cm) deep, two seeds at a time (in case one doesn't germinate) every 3 inches (7.5 cm) or so. I cover them with soil, pat down, and water.

When seedlings appear, I transplant them but don't thin them out. I harvest the outside leaves regularly, leaving the center of the clump undisturbed.

Strawberry (*Fragaria × ananassa* and *F. vesca*)

BOTANICAL FAMILY: Rosaceae

VARIETIES: Both cultivated (*Fragaria × ananassa*) and alpine varieties (*Fragaria vesca*) are available and work well in containers.

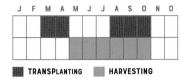

J	F	M	A	M	J	J	A	S	O	N	D
		■	■			■	■	■	■		
				▨	▨	▨	▨	▨	▨		

■ TRANSPLANTING   ▨ HARVESTING

Strawberries fall into two categories: the ones that fruit only between mid-May and mid-July and the ones that fruit twice, and that you can harvest from May-June until fall.

Even if they are possible to grow from seeds, it's preferable to start with the plants. Strawberries grow on stolons, or runners, which the plant continually produces, so gardeners often have plants to give away. Don't hesitate to ask fellow gardeners or look on Nextdoor before you purchase any.

I plant strawberry plants in small containers in the spring and/or bare roots

(runners) from July to October. I often soak the roots for about 20 minutes in a slurry that is one third potting soil, one third compost, and one third water (rainwater if possible). In French, this technique is known as pralinage and is commonly done with planting trees, shrubs, and strawberries. Pralinage has many benefits: It accelerates the healing of damaged or cut roots, it prevents fragile roots from drying out before they're planted, and it encourages the formation of small rootlets.

However, if I can't do pralinage for lack of compost, I've been known to transplant without it. I place the plant in a hole, making sure the roots are well-positioned. I fill the hole with soil, patting it down all around the plant with my palm and finish by watering. Strawberry plants are hungry for nutrients, so I transplant them into a mix of potting soil and compost, if compost is available.

Strawberries are perennial, though keep in mind that to overwinter in containers in Zones 7 and colder, you might need a cool but sheltered place (like a basement) to keep the plants during the coldest months. Just be sure to keep the plants lightly watered during winter when they're sheltered from precipitation.

Sunflower (*Helianthus annuus*)

BOTANICAL FAMILY: Asteraceae

VARIETIES: Sunflowers come in single-headed and multi-stemmed varieties. While the single-headed giants are iconic, they take up a lot of space, so if you plant a multi-stemmed variety, you—and local wildlife—will have more flowers to enjoy for a longer period of time.

I plant sunflower seeds directly into pots or trays, either scattered or in rows, making sure to spread the seeds out, at the end of April to early May. Once two real leaves have germinated, around mid-May, I transplant to the garden.

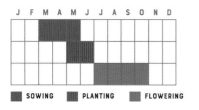

J	F	M	A	M	J	J	A	S	O	N	D

■ SOWING   ■ PLANTING   ■ FLOWERING

Tithonia or Mexican Sunflower (*Tithonia rotundifolia* and *T. diversifolia*)

BOTANICAL FAMILY: Asteraceae

VARIETIES: *Tithonia rotundifolia* is the red-orange variety of this flower, whereas *Tithonia diversifolia* has bright yellow flowers.

I plant indoors from mid-April on, in a pot or tray. I make an intermediary transplant once two real leaves have germinated, and then I transplant again in the garden once there is no danger of frost, and once the plant is about 6 inches (15 cm) tall.

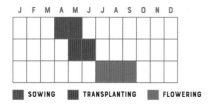

J	F	M	A	M	J	J	A	S	O	N	D

■ SOWING   ■ TRANSPLANTING   ■ FLOWERING

Tomato (*Solanum lycopersicum*)

BOTANICAL FAMILY: Solanaceae

VARIETIES: Tomatoes come in a rainbow of colors and range of sizes, from grape to beefsteak. While all tomatoes can do well in containers given enough root space, water, and fertilizer, if you have space for only a plant or two, it can be most rewarding to grow a small plant that will produce many fruits, rather than a giant variety that will put all its energy into just a few huge fruits.

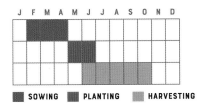

■ SOWING   ■ PLANTING   ■ HARVESTING

I start sowing my tomato seeds indoors in February. This is early, but I do it to ensure that I'll have seeds and seedlings to exchange with other amateur gardeners during springtime plant swaps. To guarantee that I have tomatoes throughout the summer, I continue sowing seeds until the beginning of April. After two true leaves have germinated, I proceed with a temporary transplant into individual pots by burying the stem up to the first leaves (cotyledons). Fifteen days before transplanting to the vegetable garden, I start to strengthen the plants by taking them outside for a short period and gradually lengthening the time they are exposed. I typically start by leaving them outside for one hour on the first day, two hours on the second day, and so on. I transplant into the garden from mid-May onward, or in rare cases, at the end of April. Just remember that tomatoes are very sensitive to cold and it's better to be safe than sorry when moving them outside.

Tomato varieties: 'Lucky Tiger'; 'Yellow Submarine'; 'Antho Gelb'; 'Tasmanian Chocolate'; 'Dwarf Red Heart'; 'Cherokee Chocolate'; 'Pruden's Purple'; 'Green Zebra'; 'Isis Candy Cherry'

Turnip (*Brassica rapa* var. *rapa*)

BOTANICAL FAMILY: Brassicaceae

VARIETIES: Turnips, like radishes, come in an assortment of shapes and colors, from long and thin carrot-like shapes to almost perfect spheres, and from snow white to deep purple. When choosing turnip seeds, you can pick a variety that allows for an early harvest to use their greens or to eat small and fresh (often called "salad turnips"), or more robust roots to cook like potatoes, which require a longer growing season.

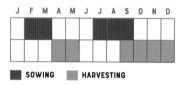

SOWING   HARVESTING

Ideally, I plant turnips straight into the garden, or in seedling trays if there's no space outside. I place two seeds per seedling tray cell in case one doesn't germinate. I cover them with earth, pack it down, and water gently to not displace the seeds. I unpot the clumps when two to four true leaves have developed, then transplant them to their permanent place in the garden. If I thin them out later, I can produce either a small harvest of turnip greens alone, which you can use as you would any of its mustard or cabbage relatives, or the leaves and a small root (an underdeveloped turnip).

Watercress (*Nasturtium officinale*)

BOTANICAL FAMILY: Brassicaceae

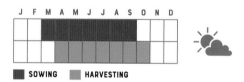

SOWING   HARVESTING

In my climate, it's possible to plant watercress from March to September, but I favor planting in spring, skipping July and August, when the heat of summer prompts the plants to go to seed, then planting again in September. Since I don't have much space in the vegetable garden, I sometimes sow in small pots on the balcony until I transplant the entire clump.

Watercress is a fast-growing plant whose young leaves can be harvested three weeks after planting. I like to pick a few leaves to add to a mix of salad greens.

Zinnia (*Zinnia elegans*)

BOTANICAL FAMILY: Asteraceae

VARIETIES: There are many species of zinnia, all native to North and Central America, but when you go to the garden center or look in a seed catalog, they will usually be classified as Zinnia elegans. Even in this one species, there are zinnias that grow almost as tall as a person, as well as dwarf varieties. There are zinnias with either tiny or enormous blossoms, and, except for blue, they come in all the colors of the rainbow—even lime green!

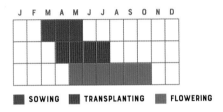

SOWING   TRANSPLANTING   FLOWERING

Zinnias are some of the easiest flowers to grow if your garden has warm temperatures and more than 6 hours of sunlight a day. They grow quickly, tolerate heat and drought, and are beloved by pollinators.

Sow zinnia seeds directly in their final growing location after all danger of frost has passed and the soil has warmed, or in pots indoors two to three weeks before your last frost. Sow seeds either 8 to 10 inches (20 to 25 cm) apart in a large container and they can grow all summer, or sow two seeds per small seedling pot for later transplanting. Cover with ¼ inch (0.5 cm) soil, then water thoroughly. Once the plants are 6 to 8 inches (15 to 20 cm) tall, pinch off the top set of leaves from each plant to encourage it to branch and grow more flowers.

The most important thing to remember when growing zinnias is to protect them from cold and damp conditions. As with tomatoes, it's better to be late than early to plant outside. (Planting zinnias out at the same time you transplant tomatoes is a good rule of thumb.)

If you live in an especially humid climate, or if your summers have many days under 80°F (27°C), you can help prevent powdery mildew on zinnia leaves by spacing the plants farther apart, around 12 to 15 inches (30 to 38 cm) to encourage air circulation.

Zucchini (*Cucurbita pepo*)

BOTANICAL FAMILY: Cucurbitaceae

VARIETIES: In addition to color variety, there are a wide range of zucchini shapes and sizes, including bright yellow and spherical zucchini.

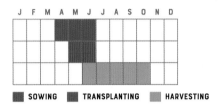

J F M A M J J A S O N D

■ SOWING   ■ TRANSPLANTING   ■ HARVESTING

I usually plant zucchini during the first days of May in a large pot. Before planting, I mix potting soil with compost or composted manure. I plant one seed per pot so that the plant has enough space to grow.

I transplant into the growing container, ideally with a minimum diameter of 12 inches (30 cm) or more, and 12 to 16 inches (30 to 40 cm) tall, after the May frost, and place it in a sunny spot. A pot with a minimum 2-gallon (7.5 L) capacity is ideal.

The zucchini—like its relatives cucumber, pumpkins, and melons—is hungry for nutrients, which is why I transplant it into a mixture made up mostly of potting soil and compost or manure. During its entire growing period, I add diluted worm tea (see page 74).

I water regularly and deeply to allow the plant to grow well while making sure to avoid watering the foliage to prevent the development of powdery mildew. I harvest the first zucchini when it's very young— about the size of a butterknife—to stimulate the plant to be more fruitful.

Zucchini flowers are also edible, and are delicious when stuffed, breaded, and fried. Use the male flowers (characterized by a slim stalk) for this since the female flowers (their flowers bear mini zucchinis) produce fruit when they are fertilized. For better pollination, I plant at least two zucchini plants. And in order to have a continuous overlapping harvest all the way into fall, I reseed in the end of June or early July.

GARDENING TOGETHER

FROM MY BALCONY TO THE COMMUNITY GARDEN

A shared garden—or community or collective garden—is typically managed by a group of people. I discovered this concept in 2013 when a square in my neighborhood was redone. After a year of construction, the project resulted in the creation of a community garden that was available to a group of residents of various socio-economic backgrounds and ages. Each person was given a plot and allowed to share the community garden's compost bins and cistern for collecting rainwater. This is how I became the happy gardener of a 32-square-foot (3 square meter) plot, thanks to which I had the chance to experiment with in-ground gardening.

As I wanted to get involved in the community garden's organization, I joined the committee of volunteers as treasurer, then director, and finally as liaison to the city until 2018. During this time, with the help of a small group of dedicated gardeners, I launched a few initiatives to hold cultural and educational events related to gardening. I enjoyed hosting workshops, an art exhibit, and picnics. We also made the community garden accessible to schools, sharing our knowledge with elementary, middle, and high school students. This is when I discovered how much I love to share knowledge. In 2016, wanting to expand my horizons and satisfy my curiosity, I went beyond the city limits to meet other urban gardeners. This is how I learned about different methods of gardening, each community garden being as unique as the people who tend it. I also made new friends along the way.

The experience of gardening in a community plot expanded my horizons, making me want to facilitate connections between people and create bonds. Thanks to the garden, I was able to interact with others as I met my neighbors, and later, city officials. Often these connections were made by children, always curious about what lay beyond the garden gate.

PASSING ALONG A LOVE OF GARDENING

As the years went by, I developed expertise and experience, and I decided to live by the third pillar of permaculture: Create and share abundance. I dreamed of forming an association to educate people about the environment. After two years of mulling it over, my friend Alice Dujardin and I cofounded the association Le Jardin Nourricier ("The Nourishing Garden").

I devote my heart to this association and use it to broadcast my passion for gardening to all, especially young people, to help them discover how vegetables grow and make them aware of seasons. I also want to teach them about the diversity of vegetables to awaken their taste buds. Take children like four-year-old Cyril, who has been coming to my gardening workshops since he was two, or seven-year-old Allan, whom I took on a tour of the garden when he was a toddler. Both of them have a heightened awareness of gardening and want to get as involved as possible.

When I joined the community garden, I was only dreaming of gardening and was a million miles

from imagining that it would reinforce my passion, give me a desire to share knowledge, and allow me to anchor myself in my community by creating Le Jardin Nourricier.

"Follow your dreams. They know the way . . ."

This quote, attributed to Kobi Yamada, takes on a special meaning now.

CONCLUSION

I dedicate this book to all those who dream of having a garden but are afraid they'll fail or won't know how to do it. I strongly encourage you to begin planting your own vegetables, fruit, and flowers, no matter the size of your space, even if you just hang pots from the windowsill.

Keep in the spirit of the proverb "The best time to plant a tree was twenty years ago; the second-best time is now." Set aside your fear of failure.

I hope with all my heart that I have inspired you and left you with the desire to throw yourself into gardening because you'll reap multiple benefits, including:

- a renewed sense of wonder at the living world, especially in the city
- an appreciation for the rhythm of nature and the seasons
- reconnecting with your food and where it comes from
- tasting the literal fruit of your labors and discovering the flavors of hard-to-find varieties
- joyfully contributing, on your own scale, to biodiversity
- enthusiastically weaving new ties with your community of amateur gardeners
- reduced stress from city life, seeing things from a new perspective, and finding well-being

These are only some of the many other benefits. Don't deprive yourself of them—garden!

FURTHER READING AND RESOURCES

Indigenous Growing Traditions

Braiding Sweetgrass: Indigenous Wisdom, Scientific Knowledge, and the Teachings of Plants by Robin Wall Kimmerer (Milkweed Editions, 2015)

Black Emu: Aboriginal Australia and the Birth of Agriculture by Bruce Pascoe (Scribe US, 2018)

Buffalo Bird Woman's Garden by Buffalo Bird Woman as told to Gilbert L. Wilson (Minnesota Historical Society Press, 1987)

Permaculture & Biodiversity

Gaia's Garden: A Guide to Home-Scale Permaculture, Second Edition by Toby Hemenway (Chelsea Green Publishing, 2009)

Introduction to Permaculture by Bill Mollinson (Tagari Publications, 1997)

Practical Permaculture: For Home Landscapes, Your Community, and the Whole Earth by Jessi Bloom and Dave Boehnlein (Timber Press, 2015)

Nature's Best Hope: A New Approach to Conservation That Starts in Your Yard by Douglas W. Tallamy (Timber Press, 2020)

The Humane Gardener: Nurturing a Backyard Habitat for Wildlife by Nancy Lawson (Princeton Architectural Press, 2017)

Carrots Love Tomatoes: Secrets of Companion Planting for Successful Gardening, Revised Edition by Louise Riotte (Storey Publishing, 1998)

Small-Space and Container Gardening

Edible Paradise: How to Grow Herbs, Flowers, Vegetables, and Fruit in Any Space by Vera Greutink (Permanent Publications, 2019)

McGee & Stuckey's Bountiful Container: Create Container Gardens of Vegetables, Herbs, Fruits, and Edible Flowers by Rose Marie Nichols McGee and Maggie Stuckey (Workman Publishing Company, 2002)

One Magic Square Vegetable Gardening: The Easy, Organic Way to Grow Your Own Food on a 3-Foot Square, Expanded Second Edition by Lolo Houbein (The Experiment Publishing, 2016)

Seeds

Seed to Seed: Seed Saving and Growing Techniques for Vegetable Gardeners, Second Edition by Suzanne Ashworth (Seed Savers Exchange, 2002)

The Seed Underground: A Growing Revolution to Save Food by Janisse Ray (Chelsea Green Publishing, 2012)

The New Seed-Starters Handbook (Revised and Updated Edition) by Nancy Bubel with Jean Nick (Rodale Books, 2018)

Online Resources

Seed Savers Exchange: seedsavers.org

Native Seeds/SEARCH: nativeseeds.org

Homegrown National Park: homegrownnationalpark.org/keystone-container-gardening

American Community Gardening Association: communitygarden.org

The Ron Finley Project: ronfinley.com

ACKNOWLEDGMENTS

I dedicate this book to my little sister Olga who left us too soon, and who gardened at her home in the Leeward Islands, in Papeete (the capital of French Polynesia).

This book is also dedicated to my niece Jeanne and my nephew Elias. I am particularly pleased that both have developed a taste for gardening thanks to regular practice, ever since they were in the cradle, then throughout nursery and elementary school.

I thank Evaine Merle, Thibaut Schepman, Arlette Tsimba, Charles Carpentier, Céline Tuo, Paul Cheam, Hella-Nawel, and Jalil Oussalah for their beautiful contributions.

I warmly thank Les Éditions Ulmer for giving me the opportunity to celebrate my passion for seeds and gardening, in particular Antoine, Lila, Guillaume, and Noémie.

INDEX

NOTE: Page numbers in *italics* refer to photos. Page numbers in **bold** following individual names of plants refer to detailed discussions about those plants.

I

insects
    biodiversity and, 81
    black swallowtail butterfly caterpillars, 116
    pests and parasites, 10–11, 57, 84–87, *85*, *86*
    pollinators, *13*, 83–84, 89
    polyculture and, 66

K

kale. *See also* cabbages and Asian mustards (*Brassica spp.*)
    growing, 21, 61, 63, 64, 84, 105
    photos, *60*, *63*, *67*, *69*, *85*, *89*
Korean mint (*Agastache rugosa*), **120**

L

lacy phacelia (*Phacelia tanacetifolia*), 83, 84, **120**
layering technique, 58, *58*
leek (*Allium porrum*), 11, 21, 45, 48, 54, 56, 84, 93, 98, **121**
Le Jardin Nourricier (The Nourishing Garden), 145
lettuce (*Lactuca sativa*), **122**
    choosing, 64, 66, 70, 71
    classification of, 98
    containers for, 29
    growth cycles of, 61
    photos, *27*, *44*, *56*, *60*, *67*, *82*, *124*, *125*
    seeds of, 44, 45, 53, 89, 90, 93
    soil for, 34
    sun for, 21
    transplanting, 54, 56–57
    watering, 76

M

mâche (*Valerianella locusta*, corn salad), 29, 64, 70, 71, 93, 98, **123**
marigold (*Tagetes* spp.), 11, 68, *69*, **123**
materials for container construction, 28–29
Mexican sour cucumber (*Melothria scabra*, cucamelon), *113*, *113*
microclimates, 11

mildew, 57, 139, 140
mint, 21, 58, 98, **120**
monoculture, 66
mouse melon (*Melothria scabra*, cucamelon), **113**, *113*

N

nomenclature, 99
The Nourishing Garden (Le Jardin Nourricier), 145

O

onion (*Allium cepa*), **126**
    classification of, 98
    companion planting, 11
    growing considerations, 16
    harvesting, 64, 71
    leeks and, 122
    seeds of, 39, 48, 93
    temperature and, 21, 45
open-pollinated seeds, 40–43
orach (*Atriplex hortensis*), 45, 48, 53, 67, *67*, 93, 98, **126**

P

parsley (*Petroselinum crispum*), 21, 34, 45, 46, 48, 64, 84, 93, *125*, **128**
peas (*Pisum sativum*), 38, 64, 70, 89, 90, 92, 93, 97, 98, **129**
peppers (chile and bell, *Capsicum* spp.*), **130**
    classification of, 98
    names for, 99
    photos, *53*, *60*
    seeds of, 38, 45, 48, 89, 90, 93, 97
    sun for, 21, 22
    temperature and, 52, 53
    transplanting, 54
perennials, defined, 61, *61*
permaculture, 5–23
    for containers, 7
    fundamental ethics/pillars of, 6, 81, 145
    "guilds," 102
    permaculture zones, defined, 14–15
    sectors, 16–17

R

radish (*Raphanus sativus*), *125*, **132**
  classification of, 98
  companion planting, 68, 70
  containers for, 29
  harvesting, 45, 64
  seeds of, 48, 68, 70, 71, 90, 93
  timing for, 71

S

safety considerations
  container placement, 31
  toxic plants, 117, 136
scabiosa (*Scabiosa* spp., pincushion flower), *42*, **132**
Scoville units (peppers), 130
sectors, 16–17
seeds. *See also* plants for container gardens, detailed information
  ancestry of, 40–43, *42*
  saving, for future planting, 89–93, *91*, *92*
  sowing process, *44*, 44–53, *46*, *47*, *51–53*
  sowing seeds vs. buying plants, 36–39, *36–39*
  timing of, 97
  volunteers, 58, *62*
self-regulation by insects, 10–11, 84–87, *85*, *86*
shallot (*Allium cepa* var. *aggregatum*), 39, 48, 98, **133**
shared gardens, 144
size considerations
  garden size, 26, *27*, *28*
  of individual containers, 29–31
snow peas. *See* peas (*Pisum sativum*)
soil. *See also* composting
  choosing and preparing, 34, *35*
  fertility of, *72*, 72–75
  transplanting and, *54*, 54–57, *56*
sorrel (*Rumex acetosa* and *R. scutatus*), 21, 48, 64, 98, *124*, *125*, **133**
spinach (*Spinacia oleracea*), 21, 45, 64, 71, 86, 89, 93, 98, *126*, **134**
strawberry (*Fragaria* × *ananassa* and *F. vesca*), 58, *60*, *61*, 64, 81, **135**
sugar snap peas. *See* peas (*Pisum sativum*)

sunflower (*Helianthus annuus*), 8, 22, 29, 83, 87, 93, **136**
sunlight, 21–22, *23*, 99
synthetic cloth containers, 28

T

terra-cotta containers, 28
Three Sisters, 102
tithonia or Mexican sunflower (*Tithonia rotundifolia* and *T. diversifolia*), **136**
tomato (*Solanum lycopersicum*), **137**
  basil and, 101
  classification of, 98
  companion planting, 68, 123
  containers for, 29, 63
  cultivars, 99
  growing from cuttings, 58
  harvesting, 64
  microclimates and, 11
  photos, *52*, *69*, *85*, *137*
  polyculture and, 66–67
  potatoes and, 131
  seed ancestry and, 40
  seeds of, 38, 45, 48, 53, 89, 90, *91*, 93
  spacing of, 70
  sun and, 22
  temperature and, 16, 21, 52
  timing of, 70, 115, 129, 139
  transplanting, 33, 54
  Twelve Core Principles of Permaculture and, 11
tools, *32*, 33
toxic plants, 117, 136
transplanting, *54*, 54–57, *56*, 97. *See also* plants for container gardens, detailed information
turnip (*Brassica rapa* var. *rapa*), 45, 48, 64, 93, 98, **138**
Twelve Core Principles of Permaculture, 9–12. *See also* permaculture

U

urban gardens, community, 144
USDA (US Department of Agriculture)
  climate information, 99
  Plant Hardiness Zones, 14, 17, *18–19*

ABOUT THE AUTHOR

VALÉRY TSIMBA is a Parisian who has long nurtured a passion for plants; her enthusiasm for gardening and thirst for knowledge led her to discover permaculture. She sets out to prove that anyone can harvest a vegetable garden with patience, observation skills, and motivation.